WILLIAMS-SONOMA

familymeals

maria helm sinskey

photography by ray kachatorian

Oxmoor
House®

contents

about this book

It was a hot and sweaty upstate New York summer day. My father was grilling steaks, occasionally prodding them with a long metal fork to test if they were done. The sun seemed to cook the tops while the flames worked on the undersides. I could hear the spit of the fat and juices as they hit the glowing coals. The smoke from the grill hung thick and fragrant in the sultry air, a light breeze every now and again swirling it into a halo above my father's head.

My brothers and I were busy shucking corn from the farm stand down the road, occasionally biting off the tip of a freshly peeled ear to taste the milky sweetness of the kernels. Our father had repeatedly told us that freshly picked corn had to be cooked as soon as possible or its sugar would turn to starch, rendering the ear inedible. Our clandestine tasting reassured us that the corn was still sweet—that we had time to get it into the pot before the inevitable happened.

In the kitchen, my mother was making potato salad from the thin-skinned white potatoes she had boiled the day before. They had spent the night in the refrigerator, and in the early morning, she had sat on the side porch and scraped the skins off with a small knife. Her salad was the picture of simplicity: boiled potato slices tossed with a handful of thinly sliced red onion, a splash of tangy red wine vinegar, a drizzle of good quality extra-virgin olive oil, and a sprinkle of kosher salt and a few grinds of black pepper. Her final touch was a hank of parsley cut from a well-tended pot, chopped coarsely and added at the last minute. Dinner was ready. We sat down together.

At a table laden with food and enlivened with easy conversation, we all vied for our favorite chunk of steak or the ear of corn with the most even rows.

When dessert arrived, fluffy shortcakes with the first sweet, local strawberries, we kids begged for more whipped cream and fruit.

This is just one of many family meals forever etched in my memory. Mealtime ensured we all remained connected to one another and to the food we ate. Cooking together was a way to communicate, whether we were exchanging stories about our day or just quietly reflecting on each other's company—all the while surrounded by wonderful smells and the clatter of pots and pans.

Nowadays, life is so fast paced that many of us have moved away from preparing home-cooked meals. As a result, we have not only become disconnected from what we eat but also to the people closest to us. Filled with creative activities and easy, delicious recipes, *Family Meals* is designed to ease you back into the kitchen with your family.

The chapters, organized by ingredients, tell you how to choose the best and freshest foods, how to identify what's in season, and how to eat nutritionally. Each chapter opens with a fun culinary project that will get your family's creative juices flowing and teach adults and children alike about ingredients, making everyone more comfortable using them. Your friends and relatives will be amazed when they hear you are curing your own bacon, smoking your own salmon, turning out loaves of sourdough bread, making homemade ricotta cheese, and rolling out your own pasta. This book promises to launch a renaissance of food and fun in your family—cooking together will be the start of a wonderful and engaging journey. A home-cooked meal will never taste as good as it will after you have put the ideas in these pages to work.

the more the merrier

Some people relish the solitary escape of cooking a meal. Not me. My mantra is "the more the merrier." My husband, Rob, and I used to man the chopping block and stove. Because we own a winery, we were constantly welcoming chefs and sommeliers as well as friends and family into our house. My years as a professional chef meant that I was used to cooking for a crowd, so Rob knew he could invite people home for dinner at a moment's notice and there would be enough food. Oftentimes, it was an unexpected, wild ride. Whoever walked in the door was handed a knife, wooden spoon, rolling pin, or salad spinner, depending on his or her skills. As we cooked with our guests, we got to know everyone better than we might have done had we relied on dinner-table conversation alone.

Our daughters, first Ella and then Alexandra, came along and were added to the mix. Initially they sat in their high chairs and watched the activity swirling around them. As soon as they showed some interest in helping, they were assigned a line on the prep list.

It started out with picking herb leaves off stems, progressed to mixing batters, and now, at ages nine and seven, respectively, they are slicing with small knives and cooking on the griddle. If you let kids help, they will dive right in!

"I'm not going to eat that!"

You might think that you will never get your kids to eat anything that isn't pasta, cheese, or white bread, so why bother with a book that introduces so many new things. That in itself is a reason. Kids shouldn't eat only white foods. Our likes and dislikes take root at an early age and sometimes linger well into adulthood. Parents shape their children's future patterns of consumption and food memories, good and bad. It's what makes our food experiences personal.

Parents wonder why their kids like buttered pasta, plain cheese pizza, and cheese sticks. The answer is simple: it is because we are the ones who are feeding those dishes to them. Kids don't starting cooking buttered pasta for themselves at eighteen months.

Parents invariably feed kids whatever meets the least resistance because food battles are a frustrating waste of time and energy. The best way to get kids to eat something new is to let them participate in its preparation. Having ownership in a finished dish instills a sense of pride and helps to make new foods less scary. The first time I allowed my daughters to make homemade fish sticks, they almost knocked me down to get to the ones they had made.

When you introduce a new food, even if your kids helped put it together, say nothing. You can praise them while they are cooking, but when the food hits the plate, smile and say "bon appétit." The minute you like something, your kids will hate it (except maybe buttered pasta). Put the new food in front of them, along with something they are familiar with, and see what happens. If they refuse to eat it, act like it is no big deal. It may take several tries—sometimes as many as ten—to get a new item accepted on their menu. Just make sure you have something on the plate you know they will eat so they won't go hungry. Enjoy your meal as you normally would—no oohing and aahing over the new food—and eventually your kids will wonder why you keep serving it and they will try it—and probably like it.

planning ahead

One of the most important things to do when attacking a meal or a project is to plan ahead. Use your chosen recipes to put together your shopping list. Make sure you have all the equipment you need and feel free to improvise. I have rolled out pasta and pastry dough with a wine bottle on more than one occasion. Plan simple meals for weekdays and bigger projects and feasts for the weekend. Every dinner doesn't have to be a three-course extravaganza. A main course with a side dish or two is perfect for an everyday supper. Some meals go together quickly and others will take a lot longer. Consider your schedule, and don't try to do too much in too little time.

roll up your sleeves

The first time your family cooks together will probably be a little rough. Just remember to stay calm, to be willing to make mistakes, and to check your inner control freak at the kitchen door. Rest assured, the more your family cooks together, the more fluid the experience will become. You will soon recognize who has a gift for washing greens or for rolling out pastry dough. Or, you may discover that your five-year-old is a whiz at measuring dry ingredients and that your husband really can make vinaigrette.

To get my family ready to cook, we wander through the local farmers' market together or stop at farm stands on weekend drives. If you don't have a backyard garden, plan a visit to a U-pick farm. Be open to buying things that aren't on your list—something that calls out to you or your kids because it smells good or is a beautiful color. Trundle everything home, roll up your sleeves, and get to work on a simple meal that everyone will enjoy.

good food and seasonality

Once we leave the family nest, we become responsible for nourishing our own bodies. Some of us are great at it, and some of us fail miserably. When you have your own family, you are in charge of making choices for everyone—at least for a while. That's when you can either opt for foods grown in a laboratory or foods that have been cultivated in soil, raised in a barnyard or pasture, or pulled from the sea. When you are feeding a family, you need to care about the origin of the produce, fish, meat, and pantry items you buy. The best market baskets aren't filled with the latest food craze. Instead, they hold just-harvested vegetables, naturally raised meats and poultry, a variety of fish and shellfish, whole grains, and eggs and dairy products from content chickens and cows.

The year-round availability of fresh foods has erased seasonal boundaries, making it harder to determine what is in season where you live. That's a shame. During my childhood, my family was almost always eating seasonally without ever having to think about it because that's what was available at a good price. Worldwide shipping was still inefficient and expensive, so we didn't have the chance to experience fruit—except the ubiquitous banana—from South America in the dead of winter.

Today, we have to work a bit at figuring out what grows where, when, and how. The best way to do that is to get to know your local farmers and purveyors or to grow your own food if you have the time and space. One of the best decisions I ever made was to plant a small organic garden and a couple of heirloom fruit trees. Every harvest seems like the first, and I constantly marvel at the beauty of the ripened fruits and vegetables. In fact, I was so satisfied with my initial efforts that I have since planted two dozen more fruit trees. Now most of our vegetables and fruits come from just outside our back door or a few miles away. My children help me in the garden, and their joy at pulling a brightly colored carrot out of the rich earth is matchless. Even if you have only enough space for a dwarf fruit tree in a pot on your terrace, plant it. It is a great way to mark the seasons.

Locally raised, seasonal foods also usually cost less and taste better than something shipped from far away. Of course you can find raspberries in December, but their taste is not worth the five dollars a basket you pay for them. No matter what part of the country or world you live in, farmers and their farms are a lot closer than you think. Use this book as a guide to choosing good ingredients and every dish will taste better.

You will soon discover that every meal will taste better, too, when the whole family picks out the ingredients, gathers in the kitchen to cook them, and then sits down together at the table to enjoy both their labor and one another.

a note on salt and pepper

I use kosher salt almost exclusively. I like its light salty taste, and it is easy to grasp with fingertips. The only other salt I use is *fleur de sel*. It is a sea salt with delicate white crystals and a fine mineral taste of the sea. I use it to finish dishes like salads and grilled vegetables, fish, and meats.

Freshly ground black pepper is my first choice when it comes to adding a spicy pop to my dishes. Its earthy flavor is best when the peppercorns are ground just before use, rather than using the pre-ground version you see at the supermarket. Once peppercorns are ground, they rapidly lose their flavor as the aromatic oils dry up. White pepper, which I use occasionally, is more refined, less earthy, and packs more heat than black pepper, so keep that in mind if you substitute one for the other.

Have fun in the kitchen!

Maria Helm Sinskey

Cinnamon rolls hot from the oven, flaky
pastries that shatter at first bite, puffy
pancakes dotted with berries—these
are foods that bring a family to the table.

breads & pastries

Flour is at the heart of every recipe in this chapter. But it doesn't
work alone. It is mixed with leavenings, sweeteners, fats, and
salts to create countless breads and other flour-based treats,
from crumbly scones and feather-light puff pastry to floppy
tortillas and crisp pizza crusts. If you've been pulling these family
favorites from the shelves and refrigerated cases of your local
supermarket, you won't need to any more. All of them are easily
made at home, especially when everyone lends a hand in the
kitchen. Teach your kids about the different kinds of flours and
leavenings, and they'll soon be popping pita into the oven
and kneading mounds of silky, elastic bread dough. And they'll
happily eat every last crumb of their floury efforts.

It seems like such a simple, basic pantry item, but add a little leavening and a handful of other ingredients to some flour and soon you will be pulling trays of delicious baked goodies from the oven.

a simple bag of flour

FLOURS FROM OTHER GRAINS

Light and dark rye, corn, oat, buckwheat, and rice flours are all great flavor and texture boosters. They are usually milled from whole grains, so none of their vibrant character is lost. But all of them are low in gluten or gluten free, which means they must be combined with gluten-rich wheat flour for most baking. Rye flour contributes a delicious sour flavor, and oat flour lends a moist sweetness. Both are popular for bread baking. Earthy buckwheat and nutty corn flours are favored for muffins and pancakes. Rice flour, both white and brown, is sometimes used for bread baking, usually with the addition of wheat flour to reduce crumbliness and provide lift.

Flour forms the foundation of every loaf of bread, dinner roll, muffin, tart, and pizza. It can be made from all kinds of grains, grasses, nuts, and legumes, but wheat flour wins the popularity contest. That's fine because wheat flour is packed with protein and nutrients, especially if you buy whole-grain flour. Most wheat flours used for baking are milled from either hard wheat, which is high in protein, or soft wheat, which is low in protein.

There are five main types of wheat flour: cake, pastry, all-purpose, bread, and high gluten, each containing a different amount of protein. Cake flour has the least protein, at just 7 to 9 percent, and high-gluten flour has the most, with at least 14 percent (see list at right). Protein content also determines which flour to use in a recipe. When flour is mixed with liquid, the protein forms gluten—stringy, elastic strands that trap the expanding gas produced by yeast or

other leavening. Gluten is what lifts baked goods and helps define their texture. Without gluten, your bread won't be soft and airy. With too much gluten, your chocolate cupcakes will be heavy and chewy.

white and whole-grain flour
A wheat kernel has three layers: the outer bran layer, the middle endosperm, and the tiny interior germ.

White flour is white because during the milling process the bran and germ are removed, taking with them lots of nutrients and good flavor. To make up for what's lost, manufacturers pump in vitamins and minerals, a poor substitute for what was once naturally there. Freshly milled white flour has a pale yellow cast. When packaged as is, it is labeled "unbleached." Otherwise, it is lightened, either with a bleaching agent or more rarely by expensive air aging, until snowy white. If you are using white flour in a recipe, I always recommend purchasing unbleached, to avoid any unnecessary additional chemicals in your flour.

Whole-grain flour is milled with all three layers of the kernel intact, yielding a more healthful product than its nutrition-stripped cousin. The bran provides body, texture, and B vitamins, and the germ, the most wholesome layer, is packed with minerals, B vitamins, protein, vitamin E, and oil—a treasure trove of both good health and good flavor. Not surprisingly, whole-grain flour is heavier than white flour and produces denser, coarser breads and other baked goods.

buying and storing flour

You can buy flour either in bulk or in bags. If you are dipping into a bin, give the flour a good look before you scoop to make sure there are no signs of insect activity. Choose flour from organically grown wheat whenever possible. It usually tastes better and is free of pesticide and herbicide residue. Flour, both refined and whole grain, should have a fresh, nearly neutral smell. Whole-grain flour, because of the oil content in the germ, is prone to rancidity. If it has an off smell, pass it up.

Store all flour in airtight containers. Keep white flour at cool room temperature for up to 3 months or in the refrigerator for up to 6 months. Whole-grain flour has a shorter life: up to 4 months in the refrigerator or 1 month at cool room temperature. Bring refrigerated flour to room temperature before using. If you see any signs of bugs or moths—everybody gets hungry—in or around your flour canister, throw the flour out.

THE TOP FIVE WHEAT FLOURS

- **Cake flour:** Low-protein flour (7 to 9 percent) milled from soft wheat. Ideal for angel food and other fine-textured cakes.

- **Pastry flour:** Medium-protein flour (9 to 10 percent) milled from soft wheat and available both in white and whole wheat (wholemeal). Great for pastry crusts and for cookies, biscuits, and other small baked goods with a crumbly texture.

- **All-purpose flour:** The cross trainer of the flour world (10 to 12 percent), made from soft and hard wheat. Use for everything from sandwich bread to pancakes to puff pastry.

- **Bread flour:** High-protein flour (12 to 14 percent) milled from hard wheat. Best for yeast-leavened bread rolls and loaves that demand a good rise and a good texture.

- **High-gluten flour:** Highest-protein flour (14 percent and up). Ensures beautiful structure for slow-rising naturally leavened breads.

rising agents

Add a bit of leavening—such as yeast, baking soda, or baking powder—to your flour mixture and voila! You can make your doughs and batters rise to light and fluffy heights.

yeast

Yeast makes dough rise. It works by feeding on carbohydrates and then releasing carbon-dioxide gas and alcohol through fermentation. The gas gets trapped in the holey gluten structure, which causes the dough to expand—this is the part kids like to watch. Yeast is happiest at 80°–110°F (27°–43°C). Temperatures above 110°F kill it. Temperatures below 34°F (1°C) put it to sleep.

Two types of yeast are used for baking, wild and commercial. Wild yeast is cultured from the atmosphere. Commercial yeast, available as fresh or dry yeast, is bought in packages at the store. Wild yeast needs a starter—a food source for the yeast—to perform: As yeast spores float by, they are attracted to a paste of flour and water. The spores feed on the flour and ferment very slowly. This unhurried action is what gives sourdough and other starter-made breads their unique flavor. Each time bread is made, a small portion of the starter is set aside, regularly fed with more flour and water to keep it alive, then used for the next batch of bread.

Fresh yeast, also known as cake yeast, is sold in moist compressed disks. To keep it from spoiling, it must be stored in the refrigerator, where it will keep for up to three weeks. It has a velvety white appearance, a crumbly, damp texture, and a fresh, yeasty fragrance. If it looks, feels, or smells otherwise, it has lost its oomph. Toss it out.

Dry yeast, which comes in the form of granules, is available in two types, active dry yeast and instant yeast. They are both still alive, but neither will act until you add moisture. Each package is stamped with an expiration date and will last at least that long if stored at cool room temperature. Most bakers reconstitute dry yeast in warm water (about 110°F/43°C) before adding it to the other dry ingredients in a recipe. It should "bloom" within about five minutes. If it doesn't, the yeast was too old, or the water was too hot or too cold. Throw it out and start again. Other bakers opt to mix the granules with the dry ingredients and then add warm liquid (up to 130°F/54°C). Just as its name implies, instant yeast works more quickly than active dry yeast, reducing rising times in half.

Fresh yeast is more temperamental than dry yeast, but if you want to give it a try, use this formula: 1 envelope (¼ oz/ 7 g/2¼ teaspoons) dry yeast equals 1 cake (.6 oz/17 g) fresh yeast.

baking soda and baking powder

Like yeast, baking soda and baking powder are leavening agents. When they are activated, they produce carbon dioxide, which causes baked goods to rise. I used to think baking soda and baking powder could be used interchangeably because they looked so much alike and yielded the same result. Boy, was I wrong. One day I made a pound cake with baking soda instead of baking powder and it tasted so bitter I had to throw it out. So, remember: they are often used together but you can never switch one for the other.

Baking soda is pure sodium bicarbonate. It reacts to moisture and acid and always needs an acidic ingredient like buttermilk, sour cream, natural cocoa, citrus, or honey to work. Once the acid hits the soda, the soda starts its rising action. That means your muffins need to go into the hot oven right away or they will fall flat. Store baking soda in an airtight container in a cool pantry and it will last indefinitely.

Baking powder is a mixture of baking soda, one or two acids, and starch (usually cornstarch, which keeps the powder dry and nonreactive). It traditionally comes in two types, single acting and double acting. Single-acting powder, which is seldom seen nowadays, contains just one acid, which reacts with moisture. The more common double-acting powder carries two acids, one fast acting and one slow acting. The fast acid reacts to moisture, and the slow acid reacts to heat. That difference gives you a little extra time between the mixer and the oven. Baking powder starts to break down the minute the can is opened, so keep it tightly covered in a cool, dry place and buy a new container after six months. If you think it might be old, test it before use: Stir a little into some hot water. If it's fresh, it will bubble.

sourdough starter

There's something in the air. At least that's what you hope when you embark on the wild adventure of making a sourdough starter. You will need patience, but you won't need special tools or expensive ingredients. The end reward is something you can eat warm from the oven, slathered with sweet, creamy butter and tangy jam—a delicious return on the time invested. What's more, you're left with a living pet that you can care for and feed for months to come.

To start your adventure, you have to capture some wild yeast in a flour paste. You don't know how long it will take or how much yeast you will trap—it takes a little more time in the winter than in the summer. Some places have a damp climate in which yeast spores flourish. San Francisco, with its famed sourdough bread, is a good example. The hunt can be much slower in drier climates, but don't despair; the starter may take up to a week to get going.

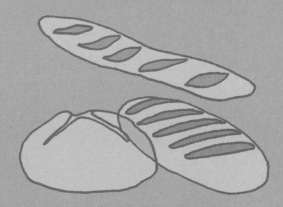

sourdough waffles

When your sourdough starter starts to overpower its home, don't throw it out. Instead, use it to make crisp, golden brown sourdough waffles. The kids can handle the batter mixing and waffle making with just a bit of adult supervision. Add blueberries or chocolate chips for extra waffle fun. To serve, slather each waffle with butter and maple syrup.

what you'll need

- 1 cup (9½ oz/270 g) sourdough starter
- ¾ cup (6 fl oz/175 ml) warm water (105°F/40°C)
- 1 cup (5 oz/155 g) all-purpose flour
- 2 eggs
- 1 teaspoon kosher salt
- 2 tablespoons sugar
- 1 teaspoon baking soda
- butter for greasing

how to make it

In a medium bowl, whisk together the starter, warm water, and flour. In a small bowl, whisk together the eggs and stir into the starter. Add the salt, sugar, and baking soda and stir until well mixed. Cover the bowl with plastic wrap and let the batter rise for about 20 minutes at room temperature. Fire up the waffle iron, grease it lightly with the butter, and pour in a scant ½ cup batter. Cook until golden brown, 3–4 minutes. Repeat with the remaining batter.

Makes 6 waffles

what you'll need to make sourdough starter

- 1 cup (6 oz/185 g) organic grapes
- 2 or 3 stainless-steel or ceramic bowls
- 1 cup (5 oz/155 g) unbleached bread (hard-wheat) flour, plus more for feeding
- 1 cup (8 fl oz/250 ml) warm water (105°F/40°C)
- coarse-mesh sieve
- two 1-qt (1-l) canning jars
- cheesecloth (muslin)
- self-sealing canning jar lids and metal-ring bands
- hammer and nail

1 squish the grapes

DAY 1 Discard any stems, place the grapes in a bowl, and crush lightly with your hands. Put the flour in another bowl and whisk in the water to make a smooth paste. Add the grapes and stir. Put the bowl, uncovered, in a warm place (about 80°F/27°C).

2 feed the beast

DAY 2 You should see bubbles in the starter and it should have a pleasant smell. If your kitchen is cold, put the bowl in a warm-water bath, or fire up your oven and leave the starter close by. Feed the starter with ¼ cup (2 fl oz/60 ml) warm water and a heaping ¼ cup (about 2 oz/60 g) flour. Stir until you have a smooth paste with grape bumps.

3 life confirmed

DAY 3 You should see a foamy sponge under an air-dried crust. (If not, your kitchen might be too cold, so try warming the starter and let it sit 2–3 more days.) Peel off and discard the crust. Whisk 1 cup warm water into the starter, then strain through the sieve into a bowl and whisk in 1 cup flour to form a thick paste.

4 your starter's new home

Divide the starter between the canning jars, cover the jars with cheesecloth, and secure each with the metal-ring bands. Put them back in the warm spot. If the starter triples in size within 4–6 hours, it is strong enough to make your bread rise.

If it doesn't, feed it each day for the next few days with ¼ cup *each* warm water and flour. If the jars get too full from feeding, discard some of the starter.

When the starter is strong enough, remove 1 cup (9½ oz/ 270 g) to make bread.

5 store it and feed it

Cover the jars, secure each lid in place with the band, use the hammer and nail to make a hole in the lids, and store in the refrigerator. Feed the starter once a week with ½ cup (4 fl oz/ 125 ml) lukewarm water and ½ cup (2½ oz/75 g) flour. If the jar gets too full, make bread or waffles (page 19), place some in another jar and give it to a friend, or throw some of it away.

crusty sourdough bread

1 cup (9½ oz/270 g)
bubbly sourdough starter

1 cup (8 fl oz/250 ml)
warm water (105°F/40°C)

about 4 cups (20 oz/
630 g) unbleached bread
(hard-wheat) flour

2 teaspoons kosher salt

olive oil for bowl

cornmeal or semolina
flour for pan

3 cups (24 fl oz/750 ml)
hot water

makes one large loaf

In a large bowl, whisk together the sourdough starter and water. Stir in 2 cups flour (10 oz/315 g) until a smooth paste forms. Cover the bowl with plastic wrap, place in a warm corner, and let rise until tripled in size and very bubbly. This will take 4–8 hours.

Add the salt and 1 cup (5 oz/155 g) of the flour to the sponge and stir with a wooden spoon. When it becomes too difficult to stir, turn the dough out onto a lightly floured work surface and knead until the dough is uniform, about 2 minutes. Gradually knead in more flour until the dough is smooth, 5–10 minutes; you may not need all of the flour. Shape the dough into a ball, place in a lightly oiled bowl, turn the ball to coat with the oil, cover tightly with plastic wrap, and place in a warm corner to rise until doubled, 4–6 hours.

Punch down the dough, roll it into a ball, and flatten it slightly into a round loaf. Pinch the seams on the bottom together tightly. Line a bowl with a dish towel, sprinkle the towel with flour (to prevent sticking), and place the loaf, seam side up, in the bowl. Cover with plastic wrap and let rise in a warm spot until doubled, about 2 hours.

Position 1 rack in the center and 1 rack in the lower third of the oven. Place a shallow baking pan with a 3-cup capacity on the lower rack and preheat the oven to 425°F (220°C). Dust a rimmed baking sheet with cornmeal.

Quickly and gently flip the loaf upside down onto the prepared baking sheet. Carefully pour the hot water into the pan in the oven and quickly shut the door. Using a very sharp knife, make 3 slashes, each ¼ inch (6 mm) deep, across the top of the loaf, and without delay, place the bread on the center rack in the oven.

Bake for 15 minutes, using a mister to quickly spray the side walls of the oven with water every 5 minutes. Reduce the oven temperature to 375°F (190°C), rotate the baking sheet front to back, and continue to bake until an instant-read thermometer inserted into the center of the loaf registers 210°F (100°C). Let cool 5 minutes, then remove to a rack and cool slightly before slicing.

Our Meyer lemon trees produce tons of lemons all winter long. That's good news because my kids never tire of this golden lemon bread. They love it in their school lunches or for after-school snacks. That means when it's time to bake, they are always willing to pitch in and zest and squeeze the lemons and butter and flour the pan. We juice the extra lemons and freeze the liquid so we can make this bread year round.

lemony lemon bread

Preheat the oven to 350°F (180°C). Butter an 8-by-4-inch (20-by-10-cm) loaf pan, and then dust with flour, tapping out the excess.

In a bowl, stir together the flour, baking powder, baking soda, and salt. In another bowl, whisk together the sour cream, milk, and lemon juice.

In the bowl of a stand mixer, using the paddle attachment, beat together the butter, sugar, and lemon zest on medium-high speed until light and fluffy. Stop the mixer and scrape down the sides of the bowl. Add the eggs, one at a time, beating after each addition until fully incorporated. Again, scrape down the sides of the bowl. On low speed, add the flour mixture in 2 additions alternately with the sour cream mixture in 2 additions, beginning with the flour mixture and mixing just until incorporated. Add the poppy seeds, increase the speed to high, and beat for 5 seconds to mix well.

Scoop the batter into the prepared pan. Bake until a thin skewer inserted into the center of the loaf comes out clean, about 50 minutes. Turn out onto a rack and let cool before serving.

get creative

Switch the flavor from lemon to orange by substituting grated orange zest and juice. If your kids don't like poppy seeds, omit them. Or, add ¼ cup (1 oz/30 g) finely ground toasted almonds in place of the poppy seeds to make Toasted Almond–Lemon Bread.

2¼ cups (11½ oz/360 g) all-purpose (plain) flour

1 teaspoon baking powder

¼ teaspoon baking soda (bicarbonate of soda)

½ teaspoon kosher salt

½ cup (4 oz/125 g) sour cream

½ cup (4 fl oz/125 ml) whole milk

2 tablespoons fresh lemon juice

½ cup (4 oz/125 g) unsalted butter, at room temperature

1 cup (8 oz/250 g) sugar

1 packed tablespoon grated lemon zest

2 large eggs

¼ cup (1¼ oz/37 g) poppy seeds

makes one loaf

My daughters and I make these breads all of the time, and our puff success rate is about 99 percent. There is usually one pita that just won't puff. The key to success is a very hot oven and a very hot cooking surface. Once you throw the dough in do not open the door until the bread is puffed.

pita pockets

1½ teaspoons active dry yeast

1½ cups (12 fl oz/375 ml) warm water (105°F/40°C)

1 teaspoon sugar

3½ cups (17½ oz/545 g) all-purpose (plain) flour

½ cup (2½ oz/75 g) whole wheat (wholemeal) flour

1½ teaspoons kosher salt

olive oil

makes 12 breads

In the bowl of a stand mixer, sprinkle the yeast over ½ cup (4 fl oz/125 ml) of the water, allow to bloom for a few minutes, then whisk until smooth. Whisk in the sugar, then whisk in ½ cup (2½ oz/75 g) of the all-purpose flour to form a paste. Cover with plastic wrap and let stand in a warm spot until bubbly, about 15 minutes. Add the remaining water, the remaining all-purpose flour, the whole wheat flour, and the salt to the yeast mixture. Using the dough hook, knead on medium speed until smooth, about 10 minutes. Shape the dough into a ball, place in a lightly oiled bowl, turn the ball to coat with the oil, cover with plastic wrap, and let the dough rise in a warm spot until doubled, about 2 hours.

Lightly flour a baking sheet. Turn the dough out onto a lightly floured work surface, and roll into a thick log. Cut the log into 12 equal pieces, and roll each piece into a ball. Place on the prepared pan, cover loosely with plastic wrap, and let rest 10–15 minutes. Position a rack at the lowest point in the oven, place a large baking sheet on it, remove the other rack(s), and preheat the oven to 500°F (260°C). For each pita, on a lightly floured surface, roll out a dough ball into a round about ¼ inch (6 mm) thick. Lay the round on your palm, open the oven door, flip your hand over, dropping the round onto the hot sheet pan, and quickly close the door. Bake until the round has puffed, 3–4 minutes. Flip the puffed round with tongs and bake until browned, 2–3 minutes more. Using the tongs, transfer the pita to a dish towel, fold the towel over to cover, and press gently with the tongs to deflate. Work carefully, as the released steam is very hot. Serve the pitas warm.

Resist the urge to open the oven door while these featherlight gems are baking and you will be rewarded with big, puffy popovers. My kids can't fight the compulsion to peek, so I always have to shoo them out of the kitchen. If you have any left over, rewarm them for breakfast and serve with jam.

puffy popovers

Preheat the oven to 450°F (230°C). In a small bowl, stir together the flour, salt, and baking powder. In a blender, combine the eggs, milk, and melted butter and blend until smooth. Add the flour mixture and blend until smooth. Alternatively, whisk together the wet ingredients in a large bowl, and then whisk in the dry ingredients until a smooth batter forms. Pour into a 4-cup (32–fl oz/1-l) liquid measuring pitcher with a spout.

Place a nonstick 12-cup popover pan on a rimmed baking sheet. Cut the 4 tablespoons butter into 12 equal pieces, and place 1 piece in the bottom of each cup. Place the pan in the oven until the butter melts and starts to sizzle and pop, about 5 minutes.

Remove the baking sheet from the oven and quickly pour the batter into the popover cups, filling them three-fourths full. Return the baking sheet to the oven and don't even think about opening the oven door for 20 minutes, or the popovers won't rise.

After 20 minutes, reduce the heat to 375°F (190°C) and continue to bake until crisp and golden, 15–20 minutes longer. Turn the popovers out and serve right away.

1½ cups (7½ oz/235 g) all-purpose (plain) flour

1 teaspoon kosher salt

¼ teaspoon baking powder

4 large eggs, at room temperature

1½ cups (12 fl oz/375 ml) whole milk

3 tablespoons unsalted butter, melted and kept warm, plus 4 tablespoons (2 oz/60 g) for the pan

makes 12 large popovers

Blueberry pancakes always remind me of long-ago summers at the beach. Suntanned and salt licked, my siblings and I would brave brambly thickets to reach the blueberry bushes that grew like weeds all over Fire Island. Back home, my father would spin the berries into fluffy pancakes dotted with sweet-tart craters of the juicy fruits.

stacks of blueberry pancakes

In a small bowl, stir together the flour, sugar, baking powder, and salt. In a large bowl, whisk together the milk, eggs, melted butter, and vanilla. Add the flour mixture and stir just until combined. A few small lumps are fine. To ensure tender pancakes, make sure you don't overmix the batter. Using a rubber spatula, fold in the blueberries. If using frozen berries, add them frozen, not thawed.

Heat a griddle or a large, heavy-bottomed frying pan over medium heat and add 1 tablespoon butter. When the butter melts and sizzles, tilt the pan to spread it evenly over the bottom. Using a ¼-cup (2–fl oz/60-ml) measure, pour the batter into the pan to form pancakes, being careful not to crowd the pan. Cook until the edges are set and the tops are covered with bubbles, about 2 minutes. Using a spatula, flip them over and cook until golden on the second sides, about 2 minutes longer. Transfer to warmed plates as they come off the griddle. Repeat with the remaining batter, adding more butter to the griddle as needed. Pass the syrup at the table.

get creative

For buttermilk pancakes, substitute buttermilk for the milk. Other berries—raspberries, sliced strawberries, huckleberries—or sliced bananas can replace the blueberries. And for an extra-special kid-friendly treat, I throw in some chocolate chips instead of fruit

1½ cups (7½ oz/235 g) all-purpose (plain) flour

1 tablespoon sugar

1 tablespoon baking powder

¾ teaspoon kosher salt

1 cup (8 fl oz/250 ml) milk

2 large eggs

4 tablespoons (2 oz/60 g) unsalted butter, melted, plus more for cooking

1 teaspoon pure vanilla extract

1½ cups (6 oz/185 g) fresh or frozen blueberries

pure maple syrup for serving

makes about 12 pancakes; serves 4–6

If your kids are like mine, they will want to watch these doughnuts puff up in the oil. Let them peek over your shoulder, safely away from the hot pan. Put them to work cutting out the doughnuts, and then let them shake the warm doughnuts with the cinnamon sugar in a paper bag that they've decorated themselves.

cinnamon-sugar doughnuts

vegetable oil for frying

2¾ cups (14 oz/440 g) all-purpose (plain) flour

¼ cup (2 oz/60 g) sugar

1 teaspoon kosher salt

½ teaspoon baking soda (bicarbonate of soda)

1 tablespoon baking powder

⅛ teaspoon grated nutmeg

1 large egg

½ cup (4 fl oz/125 ml) buttermilk

¼ cup (2 fl oz/60 ml) apple cider

2 tablespoons unsalted butter, melted

½ teaspoon pure vanilla extract

½ cup (4 oz/125 g) sugar mixed with 2 teaspoons ground cinnamon

makes about 13 doughnuts and holes

Pour the oil to a depth of at least 1 inch (2.5 cm) into a deep, heavy pot and heat to 375°F (190°C) on a deep-frying thermometer. Make sure the pot is no more than half full. Put a large rack on a large rimmed baking sheet and place near the stove.

Meanwhile, in a bowl, stir together the flour, sugar, salt, baking soda, baking powder, and nutmeg. In another bowl, whisk together the egg, buttermilk, cider, melted butter, and vanilla until smooth. Add the egg mixture to the flour mixture and stir until the dough is thick.

With floured hands, transfer the dough to a floured work surface, and knead lightly until the ingredients are evenly mixed. The dough will be loose and sticky. Pat the dough into a round 1 inch (2.5 cm) thick. Flour a doughnut cutter 2¼ inches (5.5 cm) in diameter and cut out the doughnuts, flouring the cutter as needed to prevent sticking. Or, use 2 round cutters, 2¼ inches and 1¼ inches (3 cm) in diameter. Scraps can be patted into a disk and cut again.

Using a flat spatula, carefully slide the doughnuts and holes, 2 or 3 at a time, into the hot oil and fry until golden on the undersides, about 1 minute. Using a slotted spoon, flip them over and fry on the other side until golden, 1–2 minutes. If darkening too quickly, reduce the heat slightly. With the spoon, transfer to the rack(s) to drain.

While the doughnuts are still warm, put the cinnamon-sugar in a paper bag, add the doughnuts, and shake gently to coat. Enjoy!

This tart, a summer favorite with my family and friends, tastes like it came from a pastry shop in Paris. My kids love topping the custard with handfuls of the fruit, especially ripe juicy berries, sweet white peaches, or tangy apricots. If you prefer, you can bake the fruit along with the custard: arrange it in an even layer on the top and increase the baking time 10 to 15 minutes.

raspberry custard tart

On a lightly floured work surface, roll out the pastry into a 12-inch (30-cm) round ⅛ inch (3 mm) thick. Loosely roll it around the rolling pin, and center it over a 10-inch (25-cm) tart pan with a removable bottom. Unroll the dough and fit it into the pan, pressing it against the bottom and sides and allowing the excess to extend over the rim. Trim the overhang to ½ inch (12 mm) and allow it to hang over the edge. Chill the dough in the refrigerator for 20 minutes. Meanwhile, preheat the oven to 400°F (200°C).

Prick the tart shell all over with a fork. Line the dough with aluminum foil, allowing it to overhang the edges (to prevent overbrowning), and fill with pie weights or dried beans. Bake the shell for 15 minutes, then remove the weights and foil and continue to bake until the pastry is lightly golden, about 10 minutes longer.

While the tart shell is baking, in a bowl, whisk together the crème fraîche, eggs, sugar, flour, salt, and vanilla until smooth. Reserve at room temperature.

Remove the tart shell from the oven and reduce the heat to 350°F (180°C). Let the shell cool slightly, then pour the crème fraîche mixture into the tart shell, return to the oven, and bake until the custard is set, about 20 minutes. Let cool completely on a wire rack, then remove the pan sides and carefully slide the tart off the base onto a serving plate. Mound the fruit on top of the custard and serve.

⅓ recipe **Quick Puff Pastry (page 279)**, or 1 sheet all-butter frozen puff pastry, 10 by 13 inches (25 by 33 cm), thawed according to package directions

1 cup (8 oz/250 g) crème fraîche

2 large eggs

¼ cup (2 oz/60 g) sugar

1 tablespoon all-purpose (plain) flour

½ teaspoon kosher salt

½ teaspoon pure vanilla extract

3 cups (12 oz/375 g) raspberries or 3 cups (18 oz/560 g) sliced peaches or apricots

makes one 10-inch (25-cm) tart

The extra hot oven in this recipe causes the pockets of butter to melt and produce steam, ensuring light and fluffy scones that rise beautifully. These scones are a great way to keep the kids busy. Have them measure and mix the dough, then cut out the rounds and brush the tops with cream.

cream scones

2 cups (10 oz/315 g) all-purpose (plain) flour

2 tablespoons sugar

1 teaspoon baking powder

½ teaspoon kosher salt

1 teaspoon grated orange or lemon zest (optional)

½ cup (4 oz/125 g) cold unsalted butter, cut into cubes

½ cup (3 oz/90 g) dried currants

1 cup (8 fl oz/250 ml) heavy (double) cream, plus ¼ cup (2 fl oz/60 ml) for brushing

makes 12 scones

Preheat the oven to 450°F (230°C). Line a large rimmed baking sheet with parchment (baking) paper.

In a large bowl, stir together the flour, sugar, baking powder, salt, and orange zest, if using. Scatter the butter pieces over the flour mixture, and, using a pastry cutter or two table knives, cut the butter into pieces until it is the size of large peas. Add the currants and then the cream, and stir just until the dough comes together.

Turn the dough out onto a lightly floured work surface, gather it into a ball, and knead lightly until uniform. Pat the dough into a round about 1½ inches (4 cm) thick. Using a biscuit cutter, cut out rounds. Turn the cutouts upside down and arrange on the prepared baking sheet, spacing them 2 inches (5 cm) apart. Gather scraps, pat together, and cut out additional scones. Brush the tops with cream.

Bake the scones, rotating the pan halfway through baking, until golden, about 12 minutes. Let cool slightly on a rack. Serve warm.

get creative

An equal amount of dried blueberries, sour cherries, or cranberries can be substituted for the currants. You can easily turn these into buttermilk biscuits, too. Just omit 1 tablespoon sugar and the currants, add 1 teaspoon baking soda (bicarbonate of soda) with the baking powder, and substitute buttermilk for the cream.

My older daughter prefers corn tortillas over flour, and she mastered making them at the age of seven. She even makes her own quesadillas with them. Our good friend Dolores brought us a beautiful wooden tortilla press from Mexico, which makes stamping out tortillas a breeze.

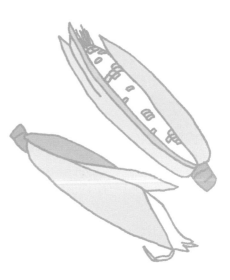

corn tortillas

Place the *masa harina* in a bowl. Add the water and mix by hand until the dough forms a stiff ball that is moist but not sticky. Add a few more drops of warm water if the dough seems dry and crumbly.

Divide the dough into 12 equal pieces, roll each piece into a ball, and cover the balls with a damp cloth to keep them from drying out.

Have plastic wrap ready if using a tortilla press, or split open a large resealable plastic bag along 3 sides, leaving the bottom seam attached, if using a rolling pin. Heat a large, heavy-bottomed frying pan or a griddle over medium-high heat.

Open a tortilla press, cover the bottom with a large piece of plastic wrap, place a ball of dough in the center, top with another piece of plastic wrap, and lower the top of the press slowly. Open the press, peel off the top piece of plastic wrap, lift the tortilla using the bottom sheet, flip it onto your upturned hand, and peel off the bottom sheet. Alternatively, place a ball between the 2 sheets of the plastic bag and roll it out into a round, then peel away the plastic and flip it onto your upturned hand.

Quickly invert your hand, flopping the tortilla flat onto the pan. Cook about 30 seconds. Flip the tortilla and cook until puffed, about 1 minute longer. Wrap the tortillas in a kitchen towel to keep them warm and pliable. Repeat with the remaining dough, and serve.

2 cups (10 oz/315 g)
masa harina

1 cup (8 fl oz/250 ml)
lukewarm water

makes about 12 tortillas

When I was a kid, my mother would bring dough home from the local pizza parlor and we would all make our own pizzas. We enjoyed those pizzas more than the ones at the pizza parlor because we had sweat equity in our imperfect, magnificent pies. And we thought the pizza we made ourselves was far superior to the pizza the parlor made. There was always dough left over, too, which guaranteed a treat the next morning.

My father would get up early and set the leftover dough out to rise. He would heat oil in a pot, cut the leftover dough into slivers and deep-fry them until puffy and golden. The fragrance of the frying dough was intoxicating, and the texture was chewy, with a craggy, golden exterior. We dusted the fried dough fingers with confectioners' (icing) sugar or dipped them in Vermont maple syrup. I remember leaning back in my chair, my smiling face sticky with syrup. I introduced my children to fried dough a few years ago, and based on their reaction, the love for this simple treat is in the genes.

All you need to make these yummy fried nuggets (similar to a beignet), are a heavy, 5-quart (5-l) saucepan half full of canola oil heated to 375°F (190°C), ½ recipe pizza dough (page 38), a sharp knife, and confectioners' sugar and/or maple syrup for dipping. Just follow my father's lead as described above.

We often have make-your-own-pizza parties at our house. I make the dough the night before and let it rise overnight in the refrigerator. The next evening, I let it come to room temperature, and then, alongside our friends, we each create our own pizza with our own personal style. This recipe is for an Italian classic, Margherita, but you can gild it any way you want—just set out bowls of different topping ingredients.

pizza dough

1½ teaspoons active dry yeast

1¼ cups (10 fl oz/310 ml) warm water (105°F/40°C)

1 teaspoon sugar

3½ cups (17½ oz/545 g) all-purpose (plain) flour

2 teaspoons kosher salt

2 tablespoons extra-virgin olive oil

makes enough dough for 4 medium pizzas

To make the dough, in a small bowl, sprinkle the yeast over ½ cup (4 fl oz/125 ml) of the water, allow to bloom for a few minutes, and then whisk until smooth. Whisk in the sugar, and then whisk in ½ cup of the flour (2½ oz/75 g). Cover with plastic wrap and let stand in a warm spot until the mixture bubbles, about 15 minutes.

In the bowl of a stand mixer, stir together 2½ cups (12½ oz/390 g) of the flour and the salt. Add the yeast mixture, the remaining ¾ cup (6 fl oz/180 ml) water, and the oil. Fit the mixer with the dough hook and knead on medium speed, adding as much of the remaining ½ cup flour as needed to reduce wetness, until the dough is elastic, pliable, and moist but not sticky, about 10 minutes.

Shape the dough into a ball, place in a lightly oiled bowl, turn the ball to coat with the oil, cover with plastic wrap, and let the dough rise in a warm spot until doubled, about 2 hours. (Or, refrigerate overnight and bring to room temperature before continuing.)

Punch down the dough, and divide into 4 equal pieces. Roll each piece into a ball, place the balls on a lightly floured plate, cover with plastic wrap, and let rest for 15 minutes.

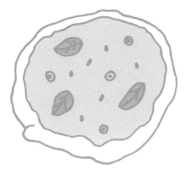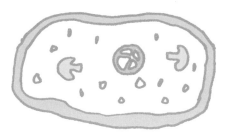

pizza pizza pizza

When you are ready to make the pizzas, position the oven rack in the lower third of the oven and preheat the oven to 450°F (230°C). Lightly dust a large rimless cookie sheet with the semolina flour.

Pull apart the dough balls, and place I ball on a lightly floured work surface. Roll out into a round about ¼ inch (6 mm) thick. Prick the dough all over with a fork and transfer it to the prepared pan.

Spread about ¼ cup (2 fl oz/60 ml) of the sauce (or less, if you don't like a saucy pizza) over the dough almost to the edge. Sprinkle with pepper flakes, if using, and then with one-fourth of the basil. Top with one-fourth each of the mozzarella and Parmesan cheese. At this point, you can add more toppings, if you like, but don't overload the dough or it will be soggy. Drizzle with oil and sprinkle with salt.

Bake until the crust is golden and the cheese is bubbling and starting to caramelize, about 10 minutes. Remove from the oven and slide the pizza onto a cutting board. Let cool for 5 minutes, then cut into wedges. Repeat with the remaining dough and toppings.

½ cup (2½ oz/75 g) semolina flour for sprinkling pans

1 cup (8 fl oz/250 ml) Tomato-Basil Sauce (page 235) or good-quality store-bought tomato sauce

red pepper flakes (optional)

½ cup (¾ oz/20 g) torn fresh basil leaves

1 lb (500 g) fresh mozzarella cheese, thinly sliced

¼ cup (1 oz/30 g) grated Parmesan cheese

extra-virgin olive oil for drizzling

kosher salt

makes 4 pizza pies

My daughters could barely contain themselves the first time they saw these big, sweet cinnamon rolls. They even insisted on each taking one to school to show all of their friends. Prepare them ahead of time and let the rolls proof overnight in the refrigerator so you can relax with your coffee and your family in the morning.

overnight cinnamon rolls

for the dough

1 tablespoon active dry yeast

½ cup (4 fl oz/125 ml) warm water (105°F/40°C)

4½ cups (22½ oz/700 g) all-purpose (plain) flour

4 large eggs

¼ cup (2 oz/60 g) sugar

2 teaspoons kosher salt

½ cup (4 oz/125 g) unsalted butter, at room temperature

½ cup (4 oz/125 g) unsalted butter, melted

½ cup (4 oz/125 g) sugar mixed with 1 tablespoon ground cinnamon

vanilla glaze (page 279)

makes 10 big, bouncing rolls

To make the dough, in the bowl of a stand mixer, sprinkle the yeast over the water, allow to bloom for a few minutes, then whisk until smooth. Whisk in ½ cup (2½ oz/75 g) of the flour. Cover with plastic wrap and let stand in a warm spot, about 30 minutes.

Add the eggs, sugar, salt, and the remaining 4 cups (20 oz/625 g) flour to the yeast mixture. Fit the mixer with the dough hook and knead on medium speed until smooth, 3–4 minutes. Add the room temperature butter and continue to knead, adding a little flour to reduce stickiness if needed, until the dough is smooth, 10–12 minutes. Cover with plastic wrap, and let rise until doubled, about 2 hours.

Butter a 9-by-13-inch (23-by-33-cm) baking dish. Transfer the dough to a floured work surface. Roll out into a 15-by-10-inch (38-by-25-cm) rectangle. Brush the rectangle with half of the melted butter, leaving a 2-inch (5-cm) wide strip uncovered on one long side. Sprinkle the cinnamon sugar over the butter. Starting at the long side covered with sugar, roll up the rectangle snugly and pinch the seam together. With the seam facing down, cut into 10 equal pieces. Place the pieces, cut side up, in the dish. Brush with the remaining butter. Cover with plastic wrap and let rise in the refrigerator overnight.

The next morning, remove from the refrigerator and let rise until half again as high, about 1 hour. Preheat the oven to 350°F (180°C). Bake until golden brown, about 30 minutes. Let cool in the pan for 15 minutes. Spread the glaze over the warm rolls and serve.

A simple, rustic galette, its buttery flaky crust filled with bubbling fruit, is a beautiful and versatile dessert. Follow the seasons when selecting the fruit. Pit cherries in the spring; peel, core, and slice apples or pears in the fall; or halve, pit, and slice peaches, nectarines, or apricots in the summer. Berries, at their best in spring and summer, should be picked over but not washed (blueberries and strawberries are exceptions).

any-kind-of-fruit galette

Prepare and chill the pastry dough as directed. In a bowl, toss the prepared fruit with the sugar, flour, and salt. Set aside at room temperature. Position a rack in the lower third of the oven, and preheat to 425°F (220°C).

Lightly butter a large rimmed baking sheet. On a lightly floured work surface, roll out the dough into a 12-inch (30-cm) round about ⅛ inch (3 mm) thick, lightly dust it with flour, fold it in half, transfer it to the prepared pan, and unfold it in the middle of the pan. Pile the fruit evenly on the round, leaving a 2-inch (5-cm) border uncovered. Dot the fruit with the butter. Fold the dough up and over the filling, pleating every 2 inches and leaving the center open.

Go back and lift each pleat and seal it with a little cold water dabbed on with your finger or a brush. After the dough has been pleated and sealed, gently press the dough against the fruit to compact it and set the pleats. Chill the galette for 20 minutes before baking to relax the dough and keep it from shrinking.

Bake for 15 minutes. Reduce the temperature to 375°F (190°C) and continue to bake until the crust is golden and the fruit is tender, 50–60 minutes. Let the galette rest for 5 minutes on the pan on a rack, then loosen the edges with a thin metal spatula. Cool for at least 20 minutes, nudging it occasionally to keep it from sticking, before serving with big scoops of ice cream.

Homemade Pastry Dough (page 278)

4 cups (20 oz/575 g) prepared fruit (see headnote)

about ½ cup (4 oz/125 g) sugar, depending on sweetness of fruit

2–3 tablespoons all-purpose (plain) flour, depending on juiciness of fruit

pinch of salt

2 tablespoons unsalted butter, cut into bits

The Best Vanilla Ice Cream (page 71) or Sweetened Whipped Cream (page 278) for serving

makes one galette; serves 6–8

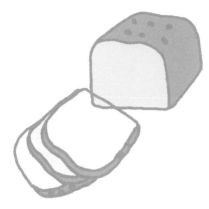

Making this whole wheat bread satisfies my soul and fills our house with the wonderful smell of fresh homemade bread. It's a great bread for breakfast toast and for the kids' favorite sandwiches: egg salad, PB&J, grilled cheese. I always make two loaves and then freeze one so I have a backup.

homemade bread

2¾ cups (14 oz/440 g) all-purpose (plain) flour

4¾ cups (1½ lb/750 g) whole wheat (wholemeal) flour

2 tablespoons active dry yeast

2½ cups (20 fl oz/625 ml) whole milk, warmed (105°F/40°C)

½ cup (6 oz/185 g) honey

2 teaspoons kosher salt

½ cup (4 oz/125 g) unsalted butter, at room temperature

makes 2 loaves

In a bowl, stir together the flours. Measure out 1 cup (5 oz/155 g) and reserve. In the bowl of a stand mixer, sprinkle the yeast over the milk, allow to bloom for a few minutes, then whisk until smooth. Whisk in the honey and salt, let stand for 5 minutes, and whisk again. Using a wooden spoon, stir in the flours to combine roughly. The mixture will be dry and flaky. Add the butter, fit the mixer with the dough hook, and knead on medium speed, adding as much of the reserved flour as needed to reduce stickiness, until the dough is smooth, elastic, and no longer sticky, about 10 minutes.

Transfer the dough to a work surface and knead briefly. Shape it into a ball, return it to the bowl, cover with plastic wrap, place in a warm spot, and let rise until doubled, 2–2½ hours. Let the kids give it the fingertip test: press the dough; it's ready when a slight indent remains.

Preheat the oven to 375°F (190°C). Butter two 8-by-4-inch (20-by-10-cm) loaf pans. Punch down the dough, cut it in half, and then shape each half into a loaf: flatten the dough, forming a rectangle 2 inches (5 cm) thick and the length of the loaf pan, and then roll up lengthwise into a loaf shape, pressing firmly as you go. Pinch the seam together and place the loaf, seam side down, in the pan. Cover the pans loosely with plastic wrap. Let rise in a warm spot until the dough is 1 inch (2.5 cm) above the rim, about 45 minutes.

Bake until the tops are golden and the loaves sound hollow when tapped, 35–40 minutes. Turn out onto racks to cool before slicing.

This thick, soft focaccia is great for making the kids' favorite panini—ham and cheese, tomatoes and mozzarella—or for slicing at the dinner table. If you prefer a thinner focaccia, use a larger pan and stretch the dough. Just keep in mind that the focaccia will double in thickness during baking.

fresh rosemary focaccia

In a small bowl, sprinkle the yeast over ½ cup (4 fl oz/125 ml) of the water, allow to bloom for a few minutes, then whisk until smooth. Whisk in the sugar, and then whisk in ½ cup (2½ oz/75 g) of the flour until smooth. Cover with plastic wrap and let stand in a warm spot until the mixture bubbles, about 15 minutes.

In the bowl of a stand mixer, stir together the remaining flour and the salt and make a well in the center. Pour the yeast mixture into the flour well, and then pour in the remaining water and ½ cup (4 fl oz/ 125 ml) of the oil. Fit the mixer with the dough hook and knead on medium speed, adding more flour to reduce stickiness if needed, until smooth, 8–10 minutes. Shape the dough into a ball, place in an oiled bowl, turn the ball to coat with oil, cover tightly with plastic wrap, and let the dough rise in a warm spot until doubled, about 2 hours.

Lightly oil a 9-by-13-inch (23-by-33-cm) baking pan or dish. Punch down the dough in the bowl, then transfer the dough to the pan. Gently stretch it to fit the pan, pushing the edges of the dough into the corners. Using your fingertips, dimple the entire surface. Drizzle the remaining oil over the dough, then sprinkle evenly with the rosemary and sea salt. Cover with plastic wrap and let rise in a warm spot for 30 minutes. Preheat the oven to 425°F (220°C).

Bake for 10 minutes. Reduce the temperature to 400°F (200°C) and continue to bake until golden, about 20 minutes. Let cool in the pan on a rack for 15 minutes before serving.

1 tablespoon active dry yeast

1½ cups (12 fl oz/375 ml) warm water (105°F/40°C)

1 teaspoon sugar

4½ cups (22½ oz/700 g) all-purpose (plain) flour, plus more if needed

2 teaspoons kosher salt

¾ cup (6 fl oz/180 ml) extra-virgin olive oil

1½ teaspoons coarsely chopped fresh rosemary

¾ teaspoon coarse sea salt or *fleur de sel*

makes 1 flat bread

The milk in the glass was ice cold. I dipped in the cookie, watched it slowly absorb the creamy liquid, and then quickly ate it before it crumbled away into the white sea.

dairy

What would we do without milk? We cook with it and we feed it to babies, pint-sized kids, and teenagers. We dip chocolate chip cookies into a glass of cold milk for an afternoon snack, and we stir cocoa into a cup of hot milk for a warm drink on a cold night. We make milk into butter, yogurt, sour cream, and hundreds of different kinds of cheeses. Then we happily turn all of these new foods into hearty lasagna, mile-high parfaits, and all kinds of sandwiches—avocado and cheese, ham and cheese, or just cheese—for school lunchboxes. And because milk is packed with protein and calcium for strong bones and teeth, vitamins and minerals for growth, and fat for energy, we sit down at the table knowing we are eating something good for us, too.

No matter if it comes from a cow, sheep, or goat, milk's potential is unlimited. All things dairy, from clouds of whipped cream and pats of salty butter to creamy rounds of brie and wedges of Parmesan, spring from milk.

the many forms of milk

Poured into a glass, milk doesn't look like much—just an opaque white liquid. And we sometimes treat it with disrespect: sneaking a drink from the carton or pouring a half-finished glass down the drain. But milk should not be taken for granted. It's both good for us and a building block for many of our favorite foods: the cream cheese on our bagels, the creamy yogurt that tops our fruit, the dollops of sour cream on our baked potatoes, the ice cream we drizzle with chocolate. And it starts with a cow, goat, or sheep.

Milk has four main components: water, lactose, fat, and protein, with the amount of each varying according to its animal source. Fresh cow's milk typically has a butterfat content of 4 percent or higher, with the amount varying according to the time of year, the breed of the cow, and what the cow was fed. A cup (8 fl oz/250 ml) of whole milk contains about 8 grams of fat. Reduced-fat milk, labeled by its fat

percentage—2 percent, 1 percent, and skim or nonfat—delivers the same benefits as whole milk with less fat and more calcium per cup.

raw versus pasteurized

Pasteurized milk was introduced in the late nineteenth century. Before then, people got sick and often died from milk processed in unsanitary conditions. But today, many people believe that pasteurization kills good bacteria and heat-sensitive vitamins, and favor the nutritional values of raw milk over the safety of pasteurized. Raw milk is safe if handled properly, so if you buy raw milk, make sure you are familiar with the producer, and keep it cold.

organic milk and milk products

Organic milk is from animals that graze on organic pastures or are fed organic silage. They must never receive growth hormones or antibiotics, and they must have access to the outdoors, though the rules don't specify exactly how much time must be spent outside. Many, though not all, studies have shown that milk and milk products from pasture-fed cows are better for you.

homogenization

If left alone, milk separates into cream and nonfat milk, and you'll sometimes see old-fashioned cream-topped milk at the market. I like the idea of the cream layer, but once it's there, it's hard to emulsify it back into the milk. The person who gets the first glass from the container gets the glob of cream, and everyone else drinks skim milk. Homogenization was developed to prevent milk frustration. It forces milk at high pressure through very small holes that cause the water and the fat in the milk to come together and hug each other.

cream

The flip side of homogenization is the separation of fat-rich cream from milk. This creates skim milk and luscious full-fat cream, and it is done commercially by centrifugal force. To do it the old-fashioned way, let milk sit until the fat floats to the top, then skim the cream from the surface; hence, the term skim milk for milk with all of the fat removed. Different types of cream have varying butterfat contents (milk is added back to cream to dilute its strength). Half-and-half (half cream) has the least butterfat, and heavy (double) cream has the most (see right). Today, most cream sold by large dairies is ultra-pasteurized, which means it has been heated to a high temperature to kill certain microorganisms and lengthen shelf life. It has a slightly "cooked" taste, and won't whip as easily as its untreated counterpart.

DIFFERENT CREAM FOR DIFFERENT THINGS

- Half-and-half (10 to 18 percent butterfat): Also known as half cream. Don't try to whip it, you will fail miserably. Stir it into coffee or pour it over your cereal for a treat.

- Light cream (18 to 30 percent butterfat): Also known as single cream. Don't try to whip this one either. Makes delicious cocoa and gives fresh fruit a rich boost.

- Light whipping or whipping cream (30 to 36 percent butterfat): Whips up nicely and delivers slightly less fat—and a lighter texture—than whipped heavy cream.

- Heavy cream or heavy whipping cream (minimum 36 percent butterfat): Also known as double cream. This is the classic choice for billowy clouds of whipped cream.

the culture club

Culturing milk makes it rich, thick, and tangy and gives it a lot longer life in your refrigerator. The best-known members of the club are sour cream, yogurt, crème fraîche, and buttermilk. Cheeses are cultured, too, but they are made by separating out the curds. Here, the curds and whey stay together, so the end product is always creamy. The culturing process is simple: Bacteria are added to fresh milk, and the milk is placed in a warm environment to encourage the bacteria to grow. The bacteria feed on the natural sugars in the milk, which causes the milk to ferment, thicken, and produce lactic acid. The acid is what gives the cultured product its tanginess. Different bacteria produce different flavors and textures. That's why yogurt and sour cream don't taste or look the same.

buttermilk

Tangy buttermilk is somewhat of a newcomer to the culture club. In the old days, it was the liquid that was left over after you churned butter. Nowadays, it is made by culturing low-fat milk. That also means that despite its name, it's not loaded with fat.

yogurt

Yogurt, like most dairy products, is packed with calcium, protein, vitamins, and minerals. Yogurt's big plus? It contains live bacteria. Studies have shown that these live bacterial cultures may help you to live longer and boost your immune system. Make sure to look for yogurt that contains active cultures. Also, if you buy low-fat unsweetened plain yogurt, you can add your own honey and fruit. It's much healthier than sugar-laced flavored yogurts—and yummier, too.

butter

The most important rule to remember when buying butter is to read the package. First, check how it is made. You'll find two basic types: sweet cream, made from fresh cream, and cultured, made from fermented cream. Sweet cream butters are about 80 percent butterfat and have a mild flavor that at its best tastes like a spoonful of fresh cream. Less common cultured butters—most European and European-style butters fall into this group—have a higher butterfat content and a more complex tangy flavor. (Pastry chefs like cultured butter because its extra butterfat makes it more pliable.) Next, check for salt. All butter is salted unless the label says otherwise. Salt is traditionally used as a preservative to lengthen shelf life, but it can also help disguise the flavor of an inexpensive butter.

Lightly salted sweet cream butter is a great all-purpose butter for slathering on morning toast or tossing with popcorn. Unsalted butter is great for baking when you want to control the amount of salt in a recipe. If you are ready to make cookies and have only salted butter on hand, reduce the salt in the recipe by ¼ teaspoon for each ½ cup (4 oz/125 g) butter.

BUYING CHEESE

The best place to buy cheese is a cheese store because the clerks typically know their products and they let you taste before you buy. But many of us don't have that option. If the supermarket is where you shop, here are some buying tips: Use your eyes and nose. Hard cheese should be free of mold. If mold is part of the cheese, it should be a uniform color. Odd-colored black or green mold or a strong ammoniated smell and excessive weeping are signals to walk on by. Use your best judgment. But if you are in doubt, look for a department worker to help.

cheese

Cheese comes in all shapes and sizes, and can be made with all types of milk. So the cheese world has simplified categorizing its big family by dividing it into four groups defined by texture: soft, which includes fresh and soft ripened; semisoft; semihard; and hard. The amount of moisture in the cheese determines its texture.

Fresh cheese is quick and easy to make. You add an acid, such as vinegar, or an enzyme, usually in the form of rennet, to milk, which then promptly forms curds. Cheese made with an acid has softer, more shapeless curds than cheese made with rennet. The curds are drained of whey—the watery part—and packaged or molded into shapes. Most fresh cheeses are not cultured, so they taste tangy sweet and even a little bland. And as their name implies, you should eat them right away.

To make soft-ripened, semisoft, semihard, and hard cheeses, you add a bacterial culture and an enzyme, again usually rennet, to milk to separate the curds and whey. The whey is drained off, the curds are salted and packed into molds to drain, and then the cheese is aged. The type of bacteria chosen, how the curds are processed, and how long the cheese is aged—from a few weeks to a few years—all help to determine the taste and texture of the final cheese. The shelf lives of these cheeses vary according to how long they are aged. Wrap them in waxed paper, slip them into a plastic bag left partially open, and store them in the refrigerator for about 1 week for soft-ripened cheeses or up to several weeks for hard cheeses.

WHAT DO I USE THIS CHEESE FOR?

- Fresh cheeses (ricotta, cottage, cream, mascarpone, farmer, quark): These naturally bland cheeses can be mixed with all kinds of ingredients for filling pastries and pastas, or for whipping up a cheesecake, or topping fruit.

- Soft-ripened cheeses (Brie, Camembert, triple cream): These are ideal table cheeses and make deliciously decadent sandwich or omelet fillings.

- Semisoft cheeses (blue, Colby, Fontina, Havarti, Monterey Jack): Use as a table cheese, in hot and cold sandwiches, and folded into omelets. The blues are great crumbled over salads or whisked into salad dressings.

- Semihard and hard cheeses (Gouda, most Cheddars, dry Jack, Gruyère, Parmesan): Just about anything goes here, from quiche and mac and cheese to omelets and pasta.

homemade ricotta cheese

Fluffy, rich clouds of freshly made ricotta: This special treat is so good you'll want to sit there with a spoon and eat it like ice cream. My first taste of fresh ricotta was in Sonoma County, California, at Bellwether Farms. The cheese maker, Liam Callahan, had just finished packing the curds for a cow's milk cheese into forms, and was heating a huge vat of leftover whey to make ricotta. He added some cream for richness, followed by salt and vinegar. It was a thrill to see the curds form in the swirling whey. Then, using a huge strainer, he lifted out the curds and handed me a few. They were warm, delicate, and delicious.

This ricotta, made from whole milk and cream, is similar in texture and taste to ricotta made from whey. Everyone in your family, from the smallest to the tallest, will be amazed to see the curds form in the pot. And equally amazed when they eat it.

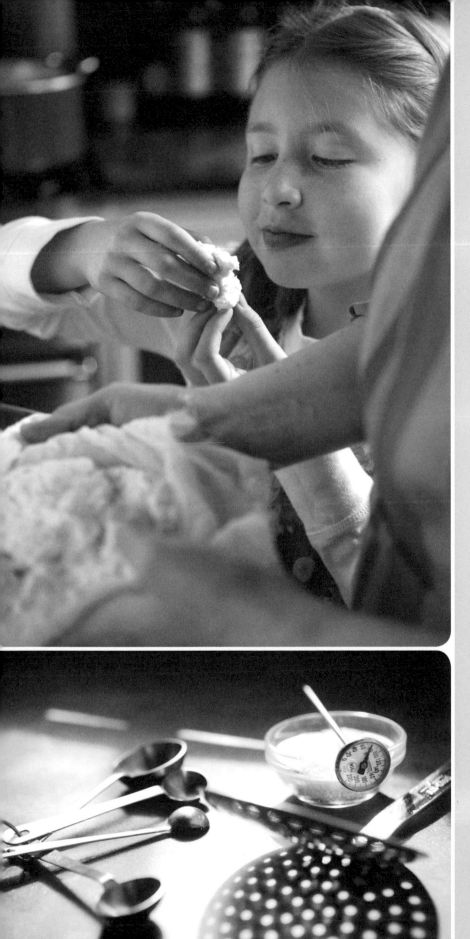

easy ideas for ricotta

Ricotta isn't just for filling lasagna and ravioli; it is super versatile and makes easy and delicious appetizers or yummy desserts.

broiled ricotta with herbed cherry tomatoes

This fresh, light starter will make both kids and adults grin with delight.

Preheat the broiler (grill). Halve 2 cups (12 oz/375 g) colorful cherry tomatoes and sauté in 2 tablespoons extra-virgin olive oil over medium-high heat just until warmed and beginning to release their juices, 1–2 minutes. Add ½ teaspoon minced garlic, 1 teaspoon chopped fresh oregano, and sea salt and freshly ground pepper to taste and toss well. Transfer the tomatoes to a shallow baking dish and distribute 1 cup (8 oz/250 g) ricotta cheese evenly over the top. Drizzle with extra-virgin olive oil and broil (grill) until the ricotta bubbles and turns golden, about 2–3 minutes.

Serves 4–6

fresh ricotta with honey and strawberries

This is a fast and simple dessert that lets each ingredient shine.

Press 2 cups (1 lb/500 g) ricotta cheese into a small bowl to mold. Invert onto a serving dish. Drizzle with 3 tablespoons wildflower honey. Surround the cheese with 1½ cups (6 oz/185 g) sliced strawberries. Serve additional honey on the side.

Serves 4–6

what you'll need to make homemade ricotta cheese

- 1 gallon (4 l) organic whole milk

- 2 cups (16 fl oz/500 ml) organic heavy (double) cream

- large, heavy-bottomed nonreactive pot

- silicone spatula

- instant-read thermometer

- ¼ cup plus 2 tablespoons (3 fl oz/ 90 ml) organic distilled white vinegar

- 1 teaspoon kosher salt

- colander

- cheesecloth (muslin)

- large bowl

- slotted spoon

- storage container

1 heat the milk

Pour the milk and cream into the pot, place over medium-high heat, and heat to just below boiling. Stir with the spatula to keep the liquid from scorching. Just before the milk boils, the surface will start to foam and release steam. Check the temperature and pull the pot off the heat just shy of 185°F (85°C).

2 make some curds

Add the vinegar and stir for 30 seconds. The curds will form almost immediately. Add the salt and stir for another 30 seconds. Cover the pot with a dish towel and let the curds stand at room temperature for 2 hours.

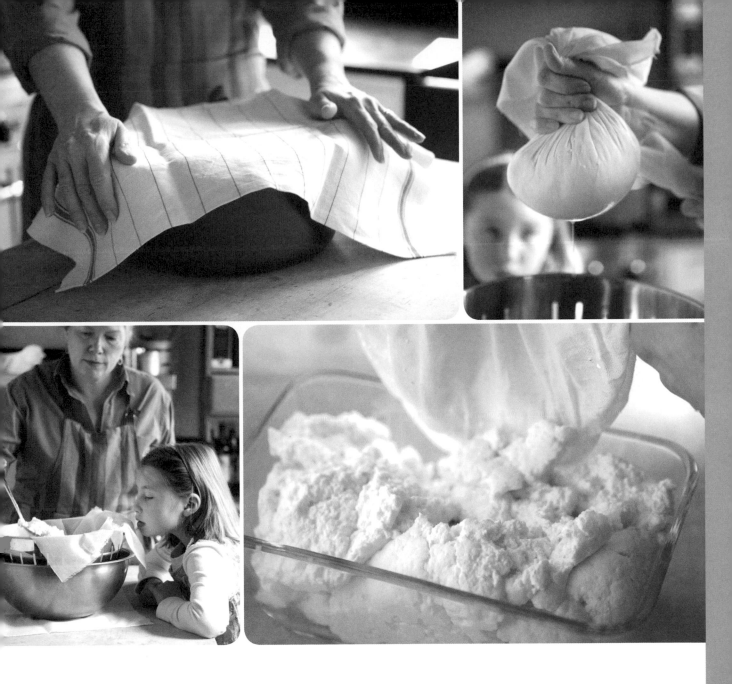

3 drain the cheese

Line the colander with a large square of cheesecloth, and place the colander over the bowl to catch the draining liquid. Using the slotted spoon, gently transfer the curds from the pot to the colander. Let the ricotta drain for about 30 minutes.

4 tie it up!

Gather the cheesecloth by its corners and twist together to force out the liquid. When the liquid turns from clear to milky and the cheese starts to push through the cheesecloth, it has drained enough.

5 store it for later

Remove the ricotta from the cheesecloth and store it in an airtight container in the refrigerator. It's best when it is super fresh, but it can be saved for up to 1 week.

Freshly made ricotta makes an incredibly light filling for lasagna. Dried noodles are no longer the only option when it comes to making lasagna. We layer thin sheets of fresh pasta with the filling and end up with beautiful, delicate lasagna. In a pinch, you can also use no-boil lasagna noodles, which are both super easy and delicious too.

extra cheesy lasagna

extra-virgin olive oil
for drizzling

4 cups (2 lb/1 kg) ricotta
cheese, homemade
(page 52) or store-bought

½ cup (2 oz/60 g) grated
Parmesan cheese

1 lb (500 g) fresh
mozzarella cheese, cubed

2 cloves garlic, minced

1 tablespoon chopped
fresh flat-leaf (Italian)
parsley

kosher salt and freshly
ground pepper

2 large eggs, lightly beaten

3 cups (24 fl oz/750 ml)
Tomato-Basil Sauce
(page 235) or store-bought
tomato sauce

½ lb (250 g) fresh pasta
sheets, homemade
(page 228) or store-bought

serves 8

Preheat the oven to 375°F (190°C). Drizzle the bottom of a 9-inch (23-cm) square pan with 3-inch (7.5-cm) sides with olive oil.

In a large bowl, stir together the ricotta, Parmesan, and all but 1 cup (4 oz/125 g) of the mozzarella. Add the garlic, parsley, 1 teaspoon salt, and a few grinds of pepper. Taste and adjust with more salt if needed. Add the eggs and mix well.

Ladle ½ cup (4 fl oz/125 ml) of the sauce onto the bottom of the prepared pan, spread to cover evenly, and arrange 2 layers of pasta, trimmed to fit as needed, on top of the sauce. Spread one-third of the cheese mixture evenly over the pasta. Top with a layer of pasta, ladle ¾ cup (6 fl oz/180 ml) of the sauce over the pasta, and then top with another layer of pasta. Repeat the layering: cheese mixture, pasta, sauce, pasta, cheese mixture, pasta, and finally the remaining 1 cup (8 fl oz/250 ml) sauce, spreading it evenly. Sprinkle the reserved 1 cup mozzarella over the top. (At this point, the lasagna can be tightly covered and refrigerated for up to 2 days or frozen for up to 3 months.)

Bake until the cheese on top is golden and bubbling and the noodles are tender, 40–45 minutes. (If baking frozen or refrigerated lasagna, cover tightly with aluminum foil for the first 30 minutes, uncover, and bake for about 30–45 minutes longer.) Let rest for 10 minutes before scooping out big gooey slices and serving.

Come winter, we head for the snowy slopes and ski all day, and then we gorge on this creamy, cheesy fondue in the evening. If you don't have a fondue pot, serve the fondue in the pot you made it in. In addition to the bread, serve sliced apples, blanched broccoli or cauliflower florets, and chunks of good-quality ham. The alcohol burns off as the fondue simmers, so kids can chow down without worry.

cheese fondue

Rub the bottom and sides of a heavy-bottomed pot with the garlic, then discard the clove. Pour in the wine, bring to a boil over high heat, reduce the heat to medium, and simmer for 5 minutes.

Meanwhile, in a bowl, toss together the cheeses and flour, mixing well. Add the cheeses, a small handful at a time, to the simmering wine, stirring with a wooden spoon after each addition until the cheese is incorporated and the mixture is smooth. Stir in the kirsch, if using, raise the heat to medium-high, and bring just to a boil.

Immediately remove from the heat and season to taste with salt and pepper. Transfer the fondue to a fondue pot, if using, and place over a warmer at the table. Place the bread alongside. Outfit everyone with a long-handled fork for dipping the bread into the hot cheese.

1 clove garlic

2 cups (16 fl oz/500 ml) dry fruity white wine such as Riesling

1 lb (500 g) Gruyère or Emmentaler cheese, shredded

½ cup grated Parmesan or grana padano cheese

3 tablespoons all-purpose (plain) flour

2 tablespoons kirsch (optional)

kosher salt and freshly ground pepper

1 baguette, cut into bite-sized chunks

serves 4–6

Nearly every child likes broccoli. Even children who won't even look at another vegetable will scarf down broccoli. I usually like it just with a bit of butter or a squeeze of lemon, but certain occasions call for something special, and this gratin is it. It is also a great way to use up those cheese ends in the fridge.

golden broccoli gratin

2 tablespoons unsalted butter

¼ cup (1½ oz/45 g) all-purpose (plain) flour

3 cups (24 fl oz/750 ml) whole milk

½ cup (1½ oz/45 g) thinly sliced onion

½ bay leaf

pinch of nutmeg

kosher salt and freshly ground pepper

1½ lb (750 g) broccoli

¼ cup (1 oz/30 g) grated Parmesan

1 cup (2 oz/60 g) fresh bread crumbs

2 tablespoons olive oil

1 cup (4 oz/125 g) mixed shredded cheeses such as Cheddar or Gruyère

¼ cup (2 fl oz/60 ml) heavy (double) cream

serves 4–6

To make the sauce, in a saucepan, melt the butter over medium heat. Stir in the flour and cook, stirring, until the mixture forms a loose ball, about 1 minute. Remove from the heat and whisk in the milk, 1 cup (8 fl oz/250 ml) at a time, mixing after each addition until smooth. Return the pan to medium heat and whisk until the mixture comes to a boil. Add the onion, bay leaf, and nutmeg and season to taste with salt and pepper. Reduce the heat to low and cook, stirring frequently, until thickened, about 10 minutes. Strain through a fine-mesh sieve into a large bowl; keep warm. You should have about 2½ cups (20 fl oz/625 ml).

Preheat the oven to 375°F (190°C). Butter an 11-by-7-inch (28-by-18-cm) baking dish. Fill a large saucepan three-fourths full of water and bring to a boil. Meanwhile, cut the heads from the broccoli stalks. Divide the heads into bite-sized florets, and then peel and thinly slice the stalks. Add 3 tablespoons salt and the broccoli to the boiling water and cook for 2 minutes. Drain well.

In a small bowl, stir together the Parmesan, bread crumbs, and oil and season to taste with salt and pepper. Add the mixed cheeses to the hot sauce, stir to melt, and then add the broccoli and cream. Pour the mixture into the prepared dish and sprinkle the bread crumb mixture evenly on top. Bake until the gratin bubbles and the top is golden, about 30 minutes.

When my husband and I were visiting Italy, we learned that it's the bread that makes the panini: the best is neither too thick nor too thin and toasts up crispy on the outside and a little bit chewy on the inside. Look for a good artisanal loaf and slice it yourself, then get the kids to help you butter the bread and stack the sandwich ingredients.

ham, tomato, and cheese panini

Preheat a stove-top panini grill, a heavy sauté pan, or a ridged stove-top grill pan over medium heat, or preheat an electric panini grill according to the manufacturer's instructions. Match up the bread slices, creating 4 even pairs, and then lightly butter the outside of each slice. For each sandwich, place 1 bread slice, buttered side down, on the work surface and layer with two cheese slices, then two tomato slices, then salt and pepper, another two cheese slices, one or two ham slices, and then two more cheese slices. Top with the remaining bread slice, buttered side up. (At this point, you can wrap the sandwiches and refrigerate them for up to 1 day.)

Working in batches if necessary, place the sandwiches in the grill and close the top plate, or place in the sauté pan or grill pan and press down firmly with a flat, heavy pot lid, pressing down intermittently. Cook the sandwiches, turning once at the halfway point if using a stove-top pan, until the bread is golden and toasted and the cheese has melted, 10–14 minutes total. Cut in half and serve right away.

get creative

Panini are super versatile, and you can make nearly any kind of sandwich using your family's favorite ingredients: tuna and Cheddar, steak and provolone, or mozzarella and tomato with pesto, to name a few. To add zip to your panini, slather on some whole-grain mustard or chopped spicy olives, or use sun-dried tomatoes when fresh aren't available.

8 slices sourdough bread or *pain au levain,* each ½ inch (12 mm) thick

3 tablespoons unsalted butter, at room temperature

24 small, thin slices Gruyère or white Cheddar cheese

8 thin slices of big, juicy, ripe beefsteak or other large tomato

kosher salt and freshly ground pepper

4–8 thin slices country-style ham

serves 4

I fell in love with homemade yogurt when I was a high-school student in France. Every few days, my French mother would plug in her yogurt warmer and culture a batch. Nowadays, I do the same for my children, who like theirs scented with vanilla and drizzled with lots of honey.

homemade yogurt

4 cups (32 fl oz/1 l) whole or low-fat milk

¼ cup (⅔ oz/20 g) powdered milk (optional)

2 tablespoons plain starter yogurt with active cultures

¼ cup (2¾ oz/80 g) pure maple syrup or 3 tablespoons honey (optional)

makes about 8 servings

Have ready eight ¾-cup (6–fl oz/180-ml) custard cups or yogurt-maker cups or half-pint (1 cup/8 fl oz/250 ml) canning jars. In a large, heavy-bottomed pan, heat the milk to 185°F (85°C) on an instant-read thermometer. Pour into a stainless steel or glass bowl and let cool to 110°–115°F (43°–45°C). Whisk in the powdered milk (if you are using low-fat milk, the powdered milk will make the finished yogurt thicker), yogurt, and maple syrup or honey, if desired; if using the latter, do not feed the yogurt to children under 1 year.

Pour into the cups, cover tightly, and place in the culturing spot of your choice: an oven heated to a consistent 110°F, a yogurt maker (set the timer), a carefully monitored 110°F stove-top warm-water bath, or on the counter in a warm place. Let stand until firm, thick, and tangy, 10–12 hours. Chill for at least 4 hours before serving. The yogurt will keep for up to 1 week.

get creative

If you plan on using the yogurt for something savory such as raita (page 65), leave it plain and don't add the maple syrup. You can also add a flavoring (such as pure vanilla extract) or a fruit compote (think sour cherry, rhubarb, or fig) after the yogurt is ready, so if you are a spontaneous person, make plain yogurt and flavor it at the last minute.

A cool, refreshing raita is the perfect thing to eat with spicy or rich foods. My daughters especially like this raita with Chickpea Curry (page 249), but it is also good alongside grilled chicken, lamb, or beef. It gets better as it sits, so make it a few hours in advance to let the flavors mingle.

cool-as-a-cucumber raita

If using regular yogurt, spoon it into a fine-mesh sieve lined with cheesecloth (muslin) placed over a bowl and refrigerate overnight, stirring the yogurt before you go to bed. When you wake up in the morning you will have about 2 cups of very thick yogurt and over a cup of yogurt water. Discard the water, and spoon the yogurt into a bowl. If using Greek yogurt, spoon into a bowl.

Peel the cucumber, halve lengthwise, and scrape out any seeds with the tip of a small spoon. Grate on the large holes of a box grater or in a food processor fitted with the shredding attachment. Squeeze out the excess water from the cucumber with your hands until almost completely dry. You should have about 1 cup (4 oz/125 g). Add to the yogurt.

Add the garlic, mint, cilantro, salt, cumin, and cayenne, if desired, and mix well. Cover and refrigerate for a few hours to allow the flavors to marry, then taste and adjust the seasoning before serving.

get creative

If you like more texture and sweetness in your raita, shred ½ carrot, peeled, and add it with the cucumber.

3½ cups (28 oz/875 g) plain yogurt, homemade (page 64) or store-bought or 2 cups (1 lb/500 g) plain Greek yogurt

1 small English (hothouse) cucumber

1 clove garlic, pressed

1 tablespoon finely chopped fresh mint

1 tablespoon finely chopped fresh cilantro (fresh coriander)

½ teaspoon kosher salt

⅛ teaspoon ground cumin

⅛ teaspoon cayenne pepper (optional)

makes about 3 cups (24 oz/750 g)

Here is a festive way to make something that's good for you and looks and tastes great. You can mix different kinds of fruits, or you and your family can create fruit-themed parfaits, such as Summer Berry Parfait or even Cherry-Almond-Chocolate Parfait—a favorite with both my kids and my friends' kids. If you don't like crunch in your parfaits, skip the granola and add more fruit and yogurt.

nutty, fruity, yogurt parfaits

1½ cups (8 oz/250 g) favorite granola

½ cup (2 oz/60 g) sliced (flaked) almonds or pecan pieces, lightly toasted

2 cups (1 lb/500 g) plain or vanilla yogurt, homemade (page 64) or purchased

2 cups (8–12 oz/250–375 g) mixed chopped fresh fruits and/or whole berries

makes 4–6 parfaits

Have ready four 1-cup (8–fl oz/250-ml) or six ¾-cup (6–fl oz/180 ml) parfait glasses or tumblers. In a small bowl, stir together the granola and nuts. Measure out ¼ cup (1½ oz/45 g) and set aside.

Let the kids help with assembling the parfaits. Divide half of the granola mixture evenly among the glasses. Top with half of the yogurt, again dividing evenly among the glasses, and then with half of the fruit, again dividing evenly. Repeat the layers, ending with the fruit. Sprinkle the tops with the reserved granola mixture. Refrigerate the parfaits for 20 minutes or so to allow the flavors to mingle, then dig in.

My family loves ice cream, particularly vanilla ice cream. No matter how many flavors my daughters sample at an ice cream shop, they always choose vanilla. One summer, I took them to New York City to visit their ninety-three-year-old great-grandmother. We decided we wanted ice cream, really good ice cream, so we walked for an hour to reach Il Laboratorio del Gelato, on the Lower East Side. The girls got tired and almost gave up midtrek, but I kept luring them with the promise of the best ice cream they would ever taste. When we finally reached the shop, my daughters seriously tasted several flavors, considered a few, and then decided on vanilla. I wasn't surprised. My younger daughter said it was the best vanilla ice cream in the world and declared it well worth the walk.

After we returned home, I made vanilla ice cream. My younger daughter tasted it and then turned to me and said, speaking very seriously, "Mom. I was wrong in New York. You make the best vanilla ice cream in the world." I immediately gave her a big hug and let her know that she had made my day.

Vanilla is our favorite, but it also makes a great base for chocolate chips, smashed ripe fruit, and scents like mint or lemon. Mix in your favorite toppings to create your own unique flavors or use it on its own for topping pies and cakes.

When I finally decided to buy an ice cream maker, it changed our lives—and reduced our ice cream bills dramatically. In addition to this wonderful vanilla ice cream, we can now pick fruit in the morning from our fruit trees and have it spun into sorbet by the end of the day. Having an ice cream maker also inspires creativity in your kids: my daughters love having their friends over and coming up with the most outlandish flavors they can think of.

the best vanilla ice cream

In a heavy-bottomed saucepan, combine the milk, cream, and ¼ cup (2 oz/60 g) of the sugar. With the tip of a knife, scrape the seeds from the vanilla beans into the pan, then toss the pods into the pan. Place over medium heat and bring just to a simmer, stirring to dissolve the sugar. Remove from the heat and steep for 20 minutes.

Meanwhile, in a large bowl, vigorously whisk together the egg yolks, salt, and the remaining ½ cup (4 oz/125 g) sugar until the mixture falls in a thick, wide ribbon when the whisk is lifted.

Remove the vanilla bean pods and reheat the milk to a bare simmer. Slowly add it to the yolk mixture while whisking constantly. Pour it all back into the pan and cook gently over medium-low heat, stirring often with a wooden spoon, until thickened enough to coat the spoon, about 3 minutes. Draw your finger across the spoon. The custard is ready if it does not immediately bleed back together. Strain through a fine-mesh sieve into a clean storage container, let cool to room temperature, and then cover and refrigerate overnight.

Pour into an ice cream maker and freeze according to the manufacturer's directions. Transfer to a tightly covered container and freeze for about 6 hours to firm up before serving.

1½ cups (12 fl oz/375 ml) whole milk

2½ cups (20 fl oz/625 ml) heavy (double) cream

¾ cup (6 oz/185 g) sugar

2 vanilla beans, split lengthwise

8 large egg yolks

¼ teaspoon kosher salt

makes 1½ qt (1.5 l)

Eggs are magical. They can be whipped into light-as-a-feather meringues, baked into silky custards for dessert, or scrambled into fluffy mounds for breakfast.

eggs

There's more to an egg than meets the eye. It is rich in symbolism: an icon of fertility and rebirth for Christians and pagans alike. It's handy, too. It comes pre-portioned and in great packaging, even if a little fragile. Eaten alone, eggs supply lots of good stuff—fat, protein, vitamins, minerals—your body needs for energy and growth. They are also multitalented kitchen performers, both whole and separated: You can stir vegetables into whole eggs for a frittata or quiche, whip the whites for a lofty angel food cake, or whisk cream into the yolks for a rich, silky custard. Indeed, eggs are an essential building block for scores of family favorites, from ice cream and cake to omelets and egg salad sandwiches.

Our family raises laying hens from a variety of breeds, which makes the population of our chicken coop colorful and exotic-looking. Every day brings a new collection of eggs in a delightful rainbow of colors.

which came first?

Even though we raise our own chickens, we still haven't figured out which egg color belongs to which of our hens, but it really doesn't matter. The eggs are beautiful to look at when lined up together in a carton. Eggs you buy at the store usually come in just two colors, white and brown, and they are nearly always from the White Leghorn and hybrids of the Rhode Island Red, respectively. But chicken eggs, regardless of color, all have the same nutritional content, unless the chickens have been treated to a special diet.

the anatomy of an egg

An egg has five basic parts: shell, membrane, chalazae, yolk, and white. The shell is made up of calcium carbonate, and its oval profile is one of the strongest shapes in nature. An egg won't break if it is squeezed with equal pressure at all points. That's why it doesn't break when a hen sits on top. The inner and outer membranes beneath the shell protect the inside from bacteria and slow down the transfer of moisture from the inside to the outside.

The yolk and the white (also known as the albumen)—what we cook—are both amazingly tough. It takes quite a bit of poking to break the yolk, and some steady wrist action to whisk the whites smooth. The yolk is also where most of the vitamins and minerals, some of the protein, and all of the fats are. Look closely at it and you'll see a small, round white disk. That tiny pool holds the hen's genetic material. Sometimes it has a little blood spot, which is harmless. Just pick it out with the tip of a spoon.

The white is the cushy ride that protects the yolk. It contains a lot of protein, which is good for us and which is why it whips up so well. The two cloudy, stringy things you see are the chalazae.

They hold the yolk in the center of the white to keep it from bumping against the shell and breaking. They are edible, but you can strain them out if you don't like their looks.

buying and storing eggs

Now that we have our own laying hens, we have fresh eggs every day. If we need more eggs than our hens are producing, we buy them from a local farmer or at the farmers' market. When I do buy eggs at the store, I choose only cartons labeled organic or vegetarian, which describes the diet of the chickens that laid them. If the carton says "cage free," it means the birds weren't caged but were probably packed into sheds. If it says "free range," it means they have access to the outdoors, but it doesn't mean they ever went outside. Chickens are creatures of habit. If they start laying eggs in one spot, they pretty much keep laying in the same exact spot. And if they are not physically put outside, they are often perfectly content to stay inside with their buddies.

Always store your eggs in the same carton that you bought them in on a shelf in the refrigerator. Those nifty plastic egg storage cases in the refrigerator door won't keep them cold enough. The soft cardboard carton also helps eggs to retain a proper moisture balance, which adds to their longevity. Some people like to store their eggs at a cool room temperature. That's fine if you consume them within a day or two. Refrigerated, they will remain fresh for up to 3–5 weeks past the sell-by date on the carton. Hard-boiled eggs will keep for up to a week.

SIZES AND GRADES

Eggs are sized according to their weight, from small through jumbo. The most popular size is large, which is the size typically used in recipes whether stated or not. A large egg weighs two ounces (60 g), with the white accounting for slightly more than half of the weight.

Quality, which is independent of size, is indicated by one of three grades, AA, A, and B. Consumers rarely see grade B eggs, most of which go to manufacturers and institutions. AA and A eggs both have clean, unbroken shells and good looks, with AA having slightly perkier yolks and thicker whites. It is a beauty contest when deciding which one makes the picture-perfect fried or poached egg.

put your eggs to work

Whether you are poaching an egg to serve over buttery toast for breakfast, whisking whole eggs to fill a quiche, or whipping egg whites to fold into a cake, eggs are the ultimate hard workers. And while they are relatively easy to manipulate, it's important to know a few basics before you get out the mixing bowl.

separating an egg

A cold egg is easier to separate than a room-temperature egg. The chill keeps the yolk and white firm so they disconnect easily.

Set up two bowls. Tap the egg sharply on its equator against a flat surface. Turn the cracked egg upright and remove the top half of the shell. Let the whites flow over the sides of the lower half into the first bowl. Carefully pass the yolk back and forth between the two shell halves, making sure you don't puncture the yolk, and allowing the rest of the white to fall into the bowl. When the egg yolk is free of the white, drop it into the second bowl. Discard the shell.

whipping egg whites

Make sure the egg whites are at room temperature. They can be beaten by hand with a whisk or with a handheld or stand mixer. Put the whites into an impeccably clean glass, unlined copper, or stainless steel bowl. Any trace of grease or fat (including a bit of yolk) in the bowl or on the whisk or mixer attachment will prevent the whites from expanding to their full volume. If using a mixer, beat on medium speed until the whites are foamy, and then increase the speed to medium-high.

To make your whipped whites more stable, add an acid such as cream of tartar or lemon juice just after the whites begin to foam. You can skip the acid if you are using a copper bowl. A protein in egg whites interacts with copper ions to create the same stabilizing effect.

If you are adding sugar to the whites, whip them until they form soft peaks, and then continue to whip as you add the sugar in a slow, steady stream.

To test for soft peaks, lift the whisk or beater. If the peaks droop, it is time to add the sugar. Once you have added it, the whites will quickly whip to stiff peaks. Be very careful not to overwhip them or they will curdle.

If you haven't stopped in time, you can sometimes save the curdled whites by adding one additional white for every three whipped whites and then whipping again just until stiff.

whipping egg yolks

Because egg yolks are 34 percent fat, they can only trap so much air, which means, unlike egg whites, they can never be whipped to lofty peaks. Also, to produce any showy volume, the protein in the yolks must be heated, such as when you make billowy zabaglione or thick hollandaise sauce on the stove top.

If you are whipping cold yolks, the most volume you can hope for is a thick ribbon, a term you often see in certain cake and custard recipes. The idea is to whip the yolks until they fall from a lifted whisk or beater in a wide, thick ribbon that holds for a moment on the surface of the beaten mixture and then slowly sinks into it. As you beat, the color of the yolks will gradually change from bright yellow to pale yellow to almost white.

To whip cold yolks, first beat them with a whisk or with a handheld or stand mixture on medium-high speed, just until smooth. Then, if you are adding sugar, add it gradually and continue beating the yolks until the mixture thickens and forms a ribbon as described above. Once you add sugar to egg yolks, you should whip it right away, as sugar reacts to the yolks if it sits for too long, causing grainy bits.

natural egg dye

You don't need to wait for Easter to dye eggs. These jewel-colored eggs are so beautiful we often have egg dying get-togethers with our friends and their kids to make them. And you don't have to rely on commercial products to create them, either. Your refrigerator and pantry hold a cornucopia of fruits, vegetables, and spices that can be turned into a rainbow of distinctive dyes.

You will need patience to produce intensely colored eggs with natural dyes, however. They act more slowly than commercial products, so you need to drop the eggs into the dye and then find an activity to keep everyone busy while the egg shells absorb the color. The first time we made these, my daughters couldn't resist hanging over the bowls of dye and rolling the eggs around, so their hands ended up as dyed as the eggs.

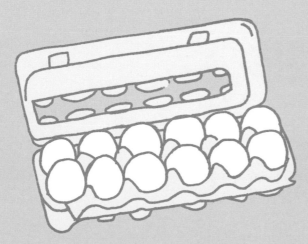

a rainbow of colors

Here's what you'll need to make
a whole rainbow of dyes:

robin's egg blue

- 2 cups (6 oz/185 g) coarsely
  chopped red cabbage
- 2 teaspoons distilled white vinegar

vivid pink

- 2 large beets, peeled and shredded
- 2 teaspoons distilled white vinegar

tropical orange

- 2 cups (1 oz/30 g) loosely packed
  yellow onion skins
- 2 teaspoons distilled white vinegar

spicy yellow

- 1 tablespoon ground turmeric
- a big pinch of saffron threads
- 1 teaspoon white vinegar

For blue, pink, orange, or yellow,
combine the ingredients along with
4 cups (32 fl oz/1 l) water in a pan
and bring to a boil over high heat.
Reduce the heat to medium and
simmer for 20 minutes to extract
the color and reduce the liquid. Let
cool and strain through a fine-mesh
sieve into a bowl. Add cold water
to bring the total to 3 cups (24 fl oz/
750 ml), if necessary.

deep purple

- 1 cup (8 fl oz/250 ml) thawed
  frozen Concord grape juice
  concentrate
- 1 teaspoon distilled white vinegar
- 3 cups (24 fl oz/750 ml) water

For purple, simply stir the ingredients
together in a bowl.

what you'll need to make natural egg dye

- **2 dozen large, white, organic eggs**
- **a large pot**
- **2 tablespoons distilled white vinegar**
- **natural dyes (page 79)**
- **as many bowls as you have different dyes**
- **newspapers**
- **old clothes to wear**
- **2 empty egg cartons**
- **slotted spoons**
- **white wax birthday candles and/or crayons**

1 how to boil an egg

Place the eggs in the pot with 4 qt (4 l) cold water and add the vinegar. Set a timer for 16 minutes. Bring the eggs to a boil over high heat, reduce the heat to medium-low, and simmer until the timer goes off. Remove from the heat, let rest 5 minutes, drain, let the eggs sit in cold water 10 minutes, then drain.

2 get ready!

Make the dyes as directed on page 79, then pour each dye into its own bowl. Protect the work surface with newspapers, and make sure everyone wears old clothes—natural dyes stain, too. Line up the bowls on the work surface, and place the empty egg cartons nearby.

3 draw on your eggs

Use a white wax birthday candle to mark the egg anywhere you don't want the dye to stick. Write a name or draw a zigzag and it will remain white when you dye the egg. Use crayons if you want a color other than white.

4 dye your eggs

Place the eggs in the dyes until they are a hue you like, usually 20–30 minutes. Using the slotted spoons, lift the eggs out of the dye and place them in the egg cartons. Allow the eggs to sit until dry, about 1 hour, before handling.

5 get dye-crazy

To tie-dye eggs, use eggs that have already been dyed a solid color, then take a brighter color, like Vivid Pink, and drizzle it on the egg with your fingertips while the eggs are still damp.

Everyone in our family appreciates a good egg salad sandwich, and it's my favorite way to use up a bunch of hard-boiled eggs. My kids like to chop the eggs up in the bowl with two table knives and mush all the ingredients together. Then, when it's time to make the sandwiches, they mound the egg salad onto the bread. If your kids yuck at "green bits," you can leave out the optional herbs.

egg salad sammies

8 large hard-boiled eggs, peeled

¼ cup (2 fl oz/60 ml) store-bought mayonnaise or Lemony Mayo (page 165)

1 tablespoon Dijon mustard

1 tablespoon chopped fresh tarragon (optional)

1 tablespoon chopped fresh chives (optional)

2 teaspoons chopped fresh dill (optional)

¼ cup (1¼ oz/35 g) thinly sliced celery

½ teaspoon kosher salt

freshly ground pepper

8 thin slices sourdough bread, toasted if desired

8 small butter (Boston) lettuce leaves

makes 4 sandwiches

The egg salad tastes better if it sits for a while before serving, so, if possible, make it a few hours ahead of time and refrigerate it. Slice the eggs into a bowl. Then, using 2 table knives, scissor-cut them into smaller pieces. Add the mayonnaise, mustard, herbs, if using, celery, salt, and a few grinds of pepper, and mix to combine evenly.

To make each sandwich, top a slice of bread with about one-fourth of the egg salad and then with 2 lettuce leaves. Top with a second slice of bread, and press down gently. Cut in half to serve.

get creative

Here are a few more ways to use up hard boiled eggs:

To make deviled eggs: Peel 8 hard-boiled eggs, cut in half lengthwise, and pop the yolks into a bowl. Cut all the measures for the egg salad in half, substituting cayenne pepper for the pepper, and add to the yolks. Mix together well. Using a teaspoon, stuff the mixture into the egg-white halves. Garnish with chopped fresh chives.

To make potato salad with egg: Make your favorite oil-and-vinegar potato salad. Pass 2 hard-boiled eggs, peeled, through a medium-mesh sieve into the salad and mix well. The eggs will add richness to the salad.

To make a mound of Ella's fluffy eggs: Shred whole hard-boiled eggs on the large holes of a box shredder-grater into a mound. Enjoy as is or sprinkle over roasted asparagus and drizzle with vinaigrette.

When I was a child, my mother frequently served an omelet and a green salad for Sunday supper, and now I often do the same thing for my family. In France, where they are served for supper, omelets are usually stuffed with seasonal vegetables, which makes them unique for the time of year. This omelet, which is delicious and simple, can be made with just herbs or with your kids' favorite cheese instead of Brie.

lots-of-herbs omelet stuffed with brie

In a large bowl, whisk the eggs until thoroughly blended but not foamy. Heat a 12-inch (30-cm) sauté pan over medium-high heat and add the butter. When the butter begins to brown, add the eggs and tilt and swirl the pan to cover the bottom evenly. Sprinkle the chopped herbs evenly over the eggs. As the eggs begin to set, using a silicone spatula, pull the edges up slightly to allow the loose egg on top to flow underneath. Continue until the eggs are almost set and no longer run when the pan is tilted.

Sprinkle with a little salt and a few grinds of pepper and remove from the heat. Add the cheese in an even layer down the center of the omelet. Using the spatula, lift one edge of the omelet and fold in half. Slide the omelet onto a plate and cut into sections to serve.

get creative

If you like your eggs more thoroughly cooked, pour the eggs into the pan and cook as directed (make sure the pan is ovenproof). Add the herbs, and place the pan in a preheated 400°F (200°C) oven until they are completely set, 4–5 minutes. Remove from the oven, add the cheese, and fold and serve as directed. The omelet will be more likely to split when folded, but will still be delicious. The options of what you can add to omelets are limitless. Some of my favorites are sautéed wild mushrooms, spinach with crumbled bacon, or blanched asparagus and fresh goat cheese.

6 large eggs

1 tablespoon unsalted butter

1 teaspoon chopped fresh tarragon

1 teaspoon chopped fresh chervil

1 teaspoon chopped fresh chives

kosher salt and freshly ground pepper

¼ lb (125 g) ripe Brie cheese, sliced

serves 4–6

The classic French salad of frisee, chewy unsmoked bacon, and a runny poached egg has been updated here with sweet cherry tomatoes and butter lettuce, making it a hit with kids who might otherwise stick their noses up at salad. It is essentially a BLT with an egg twist. Don't cook the bacon too long; you want it to be a bit chewy rather than crunchy. Have the kids grab the salad tongs and help you assemble and toss this flavorful salad.

BLT and poached egg salad

1 tablespoon Dijon mustard

1 teaspoon minced shallot

¼ teaspoon sugar

kosher salt and freshly ground pepper

4 tablespoons white wine vinegar, divided

3 tablespoons extra-virgin olive oil

6 slices thick-cut bacon, coarsely chopped

2 cups halved cherry tomatoes or 3 large tomatoes, chopped

3 tablespoons fresh basil leaves, torn

4 cups (4 oz/125g) torn butter lettuce leaves

4–6 large eggs

serves 4–6

To make the vinaigrette, in a bowl, whisk together the mustard, shallot, sugar, ½ teaspoon salt, some pepper, and 2 tablespoons of vinegar. Let the mixture sit 10 minutes, then whisk in the oil.

Heat a sauté pan over medium heat. Add the bacon and sauté until most of the fat is rendered and the bacon is crisp on the edges but still chewy at the center, about 5 minutes. Remove to a paper towel–lined plate with a slotted spoon and let drain.

Half fill a wide sauté pan with water and bring to a boil. Reduce the heat to a gentle simmer, and stir in the remaining 2 tablespoons of vinegar and 2 teaspoons of salt. Layer 3 paper towels on a plate. Keep the water at a simmer while you toss the salad.

In a large bowl, combine the tomatoes, basil, lettuce, and bacon. Drizzle on 2 tablespoons of the vinaigrette, toss to coat, and season to taste with salt and pepper. Add more vinaigrette to taste (you may not need all of it). Divide the salad among individual plates.

Working quickly, one at a time, crack the eggs into a small bowl and slide them into the simmering water. Raise the heat briefly to return the water to a simmer but do not allow it to boil. Poach until the whites are set and the yolks are still soft, 3–4 minutes. One at a time, lift the eggs from the water with a slotted spoon, blot on the paper towels, and then carefully place on the salads. Season the eggs with salt and pepper and serve the salads right away.

A morning scramble is for those days that you want something simple but plain eggs aren't going to cut it at the breakfast table. I like to cut the cheese into cubes instead of grating it. That way, the melting chunks slowly sink into the hot eggs, rather than melt away quickly.

good morning scramble

3 tablespoons unsalted butter

6 ounces (185 g) cremini or white mushrooms, trimmed and sliced

1 tablespoon minced shallot

kosher salt and freshly ground pepper

½ cup (3 oz/90 g) cubed smoked pork, chicken, or turkey sausage

6 large eggs

¼ cup (2 fl oz/60 ml) whole milk

½ cup (2 oz/60 g) cubed white Cheddar cheese

1 tablespoon chopped fresh flat-leaf (Italian) parsley

serves 4–6

Heat an ovenproof 10-inch (25-cm) sauté pan over medium-high heat and add 1 tablespoon of the butter. When the butter begins to brown, add the mushrooms and sauté until golden and their liquid has almost completely evaporated, about 5 minutes. Stir in the shallot and season with salt and pepper. Add the sausage and cook, stirring, until heated through, 3–4 minutes. Remove from the heat and keep warm.

In a bowl, whisk together the eggs and milk until blended, and season with salt and pepper. Heat a large sauté pan over medium-high heat and add the remaining 2 tablespoons butter. When the butter begins to brown, pour in the eggs. As the eggs begin to set, using a silicone spatula, pull the edges slightly toward the center to allow the liquid egg on top to flow underneath. Continue until the eggs appear about three-fourths set when the pan is tilted.

Reduce the heat to medium-low and gently fold in the mushroom and sausage mixture, followed by the cheese, keeping the eggs in large curds. You want the scramble to look velvety and voluptuous, not curdled. Slide the scramble onto a warmed serving plate, top with a few grinds of pepper and the parsley, and serve at once.

Stuffed with raspberry jam—or really any kind of good berry jam (like the one on page 102)—this French toast is fluffy and delicious and full of flavor. Ever since I turned my younger daughter on to this recipe, life on the weekends has never been the same.

french toast with jam

Working from the top of each bread slice, find the center and slice a pocket crosswise about one-third of the way into the bread. Spread about a teaspoon of the raspberry jam evenly in the pocket, and press the bread together. In a bowl, whisk together the eggs, milk, vanilla, and nutmeg until blended, and pour into a shallow baking dish. Add the bread and let soak for 5 minutes, turning to make sure both sides are well coated with the egg mixture.

Heat a large frying pan or griddle over medium-high heat and add the butter. When the butter begins to brown, spread it with a spatula to coat the pan evenly. Carefully lift the bread from the egg mixture, letting the excess drain back into the dish, and add to the pan, adding only as many pieces as will fit comfortably. Cook until golden on the undersides, 4–5 minutes, adjusting the heat if browning too fast. Flip the toast over and cook until golden and puffed on the second sides, 4–5 minutes longer. Transfer to warmed plates, dust with the sugar, garnish with berries, and serve.

get creative

To make raspberry-almond French toast, substitute ¼ teaspoon pure almond extract for the vanilla. You can also replace the nutmeg with ground cinnamon, or the raspberry jam with slivers of semisweet chocolate. Thinly sliced banana also makes a great stuffing. For really rich, custardy toast, substitute ¼ cup (2 fl oz/60 ml) heavy (double) cream for ¼ cup of the milk.

6 slices day-old white or whole wheat (wholemeal) country bread, challah, or brioche, 1 inch (2.5 cm) thick

6 teaspoons raspberry jam or your favorite jam

3 large eggs

1¼ cups (10 fl oz/310 ml) whole milk

½ teaspoon pure vanilla extract

pinch of freshly grated nutmeg

2 tablespoons unsalted butter

confectioners' (icing) sugar for dusting

1½ cups (6 oz/185 g) raspberries for garnish

serves 4–6

I often serve frittatas for weekend breakfasts because they're super easy, totally versatile, and everyone in our house likes them (plus they like to vote on ingredient combinations). This recipe offers a delicious mix of textures and flavors, with the sweet tomatoes providing a nice contrast to the earthy spinach and mildly salty feta. Other ideas: sautéed mushrooms and Fontina cheese or asparagus and Parmesan.

a colorful frittata

Preheat the oven to 400°F (200°C). Place the spinach in a saucepan over medium heat with just the rinsing water clinging to the leaves and cook, tossing and stirring occasionally, until wilted, about 3 minutes. Drain well in a sieve, pressing out the excess moisture with the back of a spoon, and chop finely. In a large bowl, whisk together the eggs and ½ teaspoon salt until blended.

Heat an ovenproof 10-inch (25-cm) sauté pan over medium-high heat and add the oil. When the oil is hot, add the tomatoes and shallot and cook, stirring occasionally, until the shallot begins to brown but the tomatoes retain their shape, 1–2 minutes. Add the oregano and season the tomatoes with salt and pepper. Add the eggs and the spinach, distributing them evenly in the pan. Sprinkle the feta evenly over the top.

Transfer to the oven and bake until puffed and golden on top, about 15 minutes. Remove from the oven, grind some pepper over the top, and serve right away directly from the pan. Or, run a thin metal spatula around the edge of the pan to loosen the frittata and, with the help of a large, flat metal spatula, slide it onto a plate.

½ lb (250 g) spinach, tough stems removed

6 large eggs

kosher salt and freshly ground pepper

1 tablespoon extra-virgin olive oil

2 cups (12 oz/375 g) cherry tomatoes, halved

1 tablespoon minced shallot

½ teaspoon chopped fresh oregano

½ cup (2½ oz/75 g) well-drained crumbled feta

serves 4–6

Quiche is a great portable meal, with endless possibilities. You can bake it, cool it, and take it with you on a picnic, which is what we often do. Unless you drop it upside down, it is quite durable. This custard filling is incredibly light, allowing the delicate flavor of the leeks to shine. Enlist the kids to help you shred the cheese and swish the leeks clean of grit (page 283).

ham and leek quiche

1 tablespoon unsalted butter

3 cups (9 oz/280 g) thinly sliced leeks

kosher salt and freshly ground pepper

1 cup (6 oz/185 g) diced smoked ham

3 large eggs

1½ cups (12 fl oz/375 ml) heavy (double) cream

pinch of freshly ground nutmeg

9-inch (23-cm) partially baked pie shell (page 278)

¼ cup (1 oz/30 g) finely shredded Gruyère cheese

makes one 9-inch (23-cm) quiche

In a large sauté pan, melt the butter over medium-high heat until it turns golden. Add the leeks and sauté until wilted but still bright green, about 2 minutes. Season with salt and pepper and turn out onto a baking sheet to cool. Transfer to a bowl and stir in the ham.

Preheat the oven to 350°F (180°C). In a large bowl, whisk together the eggs and cream. Season with ½ teaspoon salt, a grind or two of pepper, and the nutmeg. Scatter the leek mixture evenly over the bottom of the pastry shell. Pour in the egg mixture and mix lightly with a fork to distribute evenly. Sprinkle evenly with the cheese.

Bake until the custard is set and the top is golden, 40–45 minutes. If the custard is set but the top has not turned golden brown, slip the quiche under the broiler (grill) for 1–2 minutes, watching closely. Let cool about 20 minutes on a rack before serving.

get creative

Instead of a classic round quiche, divide the filling between two 13-by-4-inch (33-by-10-cm) rectangular, partially baked tart shells. All types of vegetables and cheeses can be combined and used in the quiche filling. It is a great way to use up leftovers. Some of our favorite combinations are blanched cauliflower with Parmesan and artichoke hearts with goat cheese.

This pancake is so unbelievably puffy that you will have to make sure the kids see the before and after: when it goes into the oven and then again the moment it emerges sky high. I get excited every time I make it. The tangy apples pair perfectly with the custardy texture of the pancake.

puffy apple oven pancake

2 Fuji apples or other baking apples

⅔ cup (3½ oz/105 g) all-purpose (plain) flour

½ teaspoon ground cinnamon

2 tablespoons granulated sugar

¼ teaspoon kosher salt

4 large eggs

1 cup (8 fl oz/250 ml) whole milk

1 teaspoon pure vanilla extract

2 tablespoons unsalted butter, melted and cooled, plus 4 tablespoons (2 oz/60 g)

confectioners' (icing) sugar for dusting

serves 4–6

Preheat the oven to 425°F (220°C). Peel, halve, and core the apples, and cut each apple into 16 wedges. In a small bowl, stir together the flour, cinnamon, granulated sugar, and salt. In a blender, combine the eggs, milk, vanilla, and the 2 tablespoons melted butter and process just until smooth. Add the flour mixture and blend just enough to make a smooth batter.

In an ovenproof 10-inch (25-cm) sauté pan, melt 3 tablespoons of the butter over medium-high heat. When the butter begins to brown, add the apples and cook, turning as needed, until golden on all sides, about 5 minutes. Add the remaining 1 tablespoon butter and heat until it is melted and bubbling. Pour the batter over the apples and immediately transfer the pan to the oven.

Bake until puffed and golden, 15–20 minutes. Dust with confectioners' sugar and serve the pancake directly from the pan.

get creative

For a pear-almond pancake, use 2 pears in place of the apples and pure almond extract in place of the vanilla, then sprinkle ¼ cup (1 oz/28 g) sliced (flaked) almonds on top before baking.

I remember as a child holding a monstrous wedge of this cake in my hand and stuffing the sweet and airy cake into my mouth. Let your kids watch you beat the egg whites; they will be amazed at how they transform from liquid goo to big, fluffy white clouds.

angel food cake

Position a rack in the lower third of the oven, making sure there is plenty of headroom for the cake, and preheat the oven to 350°F (180°C). Have ready an ungreased 10-inch (25-cm) angel food cake pan.

In a small bowl, sift together the confectioners' sugar and flour. In the bowl of a stand mixer, using the whisk attachment, beat the egg whites, cream of tartar, and salt at medium speed until foamy. Increase the speed to high, then slowly pour in the granulated sugar, beating just until soft peaks form. Add the vanilla and almond extracts and beat for 30 seconds longer, just until stiff peaks form. Do not overbeat.

Using a rubber spatula, scrape the beaten egg whites into an oversized bowl. Gently and quickly fold the flour mixture into the egg whites in 3 equal batches, making sure no pockets of flour remain. Scoop the batter into the cake pan and smooth the top. Tap the pan lightly against the counter to remove any large air pockets.

Bake until golden and puffed and a thin skewer inserted near the center comes out clean, 40–45 minutes. Remove from the oven, let cool for 5 minutes, and then invert the pan onto its feet or over the neck of a wine bottle and let cool completely. To unmold, run a long, thin knife blade around the inside of the pan and the tube to loosen the cake. Invert the pan and tap gently until the cake slides out.

½ cup (2 oz/60 g) confectioners' (icing) sugar

1 cup (4 oz/125 g) cake (soft-wheat) flour

2 cups (16 fl oz/500 ml) egg whites (from about 14 large eggs), at room temperature

2 teaspoons cream of tartar

½ teaspoon kosher salt

1½ cups (12 oz/375 g) granulated sugar

1 teaspoon pure vanilla extract

½ teaspoon pure almond extract

makes one 10-inch (25-cm) cake

Whether a sweet spring strawberry, a juicy summer peach, a crisp autumn apple, or a bright winter tangerine, fragrant, ripe fruit is one of the best indicators of the season.

fruit

Fruits are the stuff of history: Baskets of figs were found in Egyptian tombs alongside the mummies. And they are the stuff of fairy tales: Snow White couldn't resist the poisoned apple offered by the queen. They are beautiful to look at, wonderfully fragrant when ripe, and conceal an assortment of vitamins, minerals, fiber, and complex carbohydrates, all served up in a single sensational package. They also seem to sense our mood. Just when we start to tire of one season's fruits, another season begins with an abundance of sweet, juicy choices for tucking into turnovers, baking under a cobbler crust, roasting in the oven, whipping up into smoothies, or just eating out of hand.

Whether it is sliced, baked, layered, or eaten out of hand, my family loves fruit. From berries and apricots to mango and pears, sweet, succulent fruit is the perfect treat: it's healthy, in tune with the seasons, and has amazing variety.

a delicious and nutritious rainbow

We are lucky to have a rainbow of fruits at our fingertips. Most of them are sweet and fragrant, making them nearly irresistible. Even fruits that aren't inherently sweet, such as those that have more in common with vegetables, are enticing. Who can pass up the rich, creamy flesh of an avocado, or the juicy pulp of a sun-ripened tomato? Kids might have to be force-fed vegetables, but the same is seldom true of fruit. And that's a good thing because fruits are rich in carbohydrates, fiber, potassium, and vitamins A and C. Some even contain respectable amounts of iron and calcium.

the rhythm of seasonal fruit

The best way to enjoy most fruits is raw and at their peak of season. Some fruits, such as apples, oranges, grapes, and berries, are often in the market year-round. But at some point during those twelve months, these always-present fruits were brought in from halfway around the world. Sometimes those long travelers taste pretty good, but do you want to buy them? They are usually picked underripe so they'll last during their lengthy journey. That means they will never taste their best.

There is a rhythm to the ripening of fruit that we often miss nowadays because of imports from the southern hemisphere. I try to avoid being distracted by imported fruits and instead stay focused on what we have at hand. After a long winter of citrus and of exotics shipped in from the tropics, I am eager for the first strawberries. Their arrival at the farm stands along California country roads signals that spring is finally here and summer is heading our way. As the last lemons disappear from our tree, tart stalks of rhubarb are finally ripe enough to join the strawberries in the first pairing of spring, an interesting match between a fruit and a vegetable masquerading as a fruit.

Cherries and apricots arrive next on the scene. They straddle the boundaries of summer and spring and announce the arrival of the stone fruit season. Sour cherries are fleeting in mid-May. If you find them, buy them and spin them into turnovers and pie. Their sweet sisters, deep ruby Bings and blush red and yellow Rainiers, quickly replace them. This burst of early stone fruit slides into plums, peaches, and nectarines as summer advances. Figs make a short appearance and then quickly return to the wings to await their main entrance in the fall.

Raspberries and blueberries arrive at our markets just in time for the Fourth of July. Summer brings big bowls of fruit salad, pies, and crumbles. Dust off the ice cream machine and spin sweet fruit purée into sorbet. Melons finally ripen midsummer, and July and August keep pushing out a fruit basket piled high with berries, peaches, nectarines, plums, and melons. The early apples of mid-August remind us that fall is on its way.

The pomes—apples, pears, quince—tumble forth at the start of September. Our fruit choices wane by the end of October, with only pomegranates and persimmons to take us into November. By the time the persimmons have said their last good-bye, we will start our feast of sweet oranges, grapefruits, lemons, and tangerines, and the seasonal cycle will begin again. Local citrus will be joined by a cornucopia of tropical fruits whose season arrives as temperatures drop. Throughout all of this we have the stodgy permanence of bananas—our backup if all else fails.

SPRING FRUITS

cherries

strawberries

late citrus: lemons, limes, grapefruit, oranges, tangerines

early apricots

manila mangoes

FALL FRUITS

apples

pears

figs

quinces

grapes

pomegranates

persimmons

SUMMER FRUITS

raspberries

blueberries

blackberries

early figs

apricots

peaches

nectarines

plums

pluots

melons

WINTER FRUITS

oranges

tangerines

grapefruits

lemons

limes

kiwi

kumquats

pineapples

mangoes

papayas

buying the freshest fruits

The freshest fruits are grown locally and sold at farmers' markets, farm stands, and some grocery stores and produce markets. Look for bins filled to overflowing with beautiful, ripe fruits at a good price. That usually means they are in season. Shop only for what you need for a few days. Fruit is perishable and most types, with the exception of apples and pears, don't benefit from refrigeration. Smell the fruit as you select it. Ripe fruit smells fragrant. The skin should be smooth and free of serious pits and bruising. Superficial blemishes are fine. Skip fruits with an off smell or with any sign of shriveling. Berries should be plump and not mashed, and no juice should be dripping from the bottom of the basket.

I buy organic fruit whenever possible to avoid pesticide residue and because I am assured of good farming practices. Many times I buy local fruit that is not certified organic. I know the farmers and how they grow their crops. If you are at the farmers' market and are unsure of how a vendor's fruit is grown, ask whether the fruit is organic and what, if any, sprays are used on it. If you are in doubt about spray, peel fruits before eating them. Washing removes dirt but not much more.

Sometimes you will see fruits labeled heirloom. This does not tell you how they were grown. What it does tell you is that the variety was probably first cultivated at least fifty years ago.

Apples and pears are at the forefront of this heirloom movement, but apricots, cherries, peaches, and quinces are not far behind. In the past, many more cultivars of each type of fruit were available to cooks. In other words, you bought a different apple variety for pies and tarts, for cider, for sauce, for candying, and for eating out of hand. Today, it is rare to see more than three or four different apple varieties at the supermarket, and what you see are so-called all-purpose apples—good for pies or for eating out of hand—with good shelf life. Try heirlooms when you can to experience a spectrum of flavors and textures.

when you get it home

As soon as you return home, remove fruits from their bags. They need to breathe. Tender fruits that bruise easily, such as apricots and peaches, should be stored in a single layer, such as on a baking sheet. Store uncut fruit at room temperature. Cut fruit can go into the refrigerator because the fruit will not ripen further once cut. To store berries, spread a clean cloth on a tray and arrange the berries in a single layer. Cover them with another cloth, and place in the refrigerator. The berries will keep for up to a week. Do not wash fruits until just before you are going to eat them. Once washed, they begin to deteriorate rapidly.

a pick-your-own story

When I was a kid, I remember struggling to shove a narrow triangular ladder into a tree at the pick-your-own apple farm

HIGH PESTICIDE FRUITS

This list contains the top twelve fruits that contain the highest pesticide residue, listed in order of highest pesticide load:

peaches

apples

nectarines

strawberries

cherries

imported grapes

pears

raspberries

plums

oranges

domestic grapes

tangerines

(Source: Environmental Working Group)

our family visited each fall. Once my father made sure the ladder was safely anchored, we would all gorge ourselves on sweet sun-warmed apples as we picked, and our faces and arms, sticky with juice, would draw swarms of wasps. When our bags were brimming with apples, we would head home to make apple pies, applesauce, and apple-sparked salads. Picking apples on a crisp fall day and enjoying the delicious rewards of our labor made us happy.

I returned to the same orchard twenty years later to find that all of the trees were barely taller than I was and there was no ladder in sight. I was disappointed. Gone was the challenge of trying to reach apples on the top branches just beyond my grasp. The reasons? People were dropping from the trees along with the apples, and shorter trees made picking easier. I still appreciate freshly picked fruit, but the sense of adventure is now only a memory.

very berry jam

Raspberry, blackberry, blueberry, strawberry, mulberry—choose the berry, then follow a few simple steps to make sweet, fresh jam in less than an hour. Then, when you open a jar in the dead of winter, it will remind you of sunny summer days.

You don't need any special equipment or ingredients. One grated green apple, skin and all, provides enough pectin to set the jam, plus it adds flavor. You don't need to sterilize jars or process the jam in hot water. Just fill clean jars with hot jam, cover them, flip them over, and let the molten jam sterilize the lids and create a vacuum.

Use ripe but not overripe fruit. Have younger kids pick through the berries, mash them to a pulp with the sugar right in the pot, and design their own jar labels. Adults or teenagers can stir the pot, watching out for spatters when the jam is hot, and ladle the jam into the jars.

the pectin connection

All fruits contain pectin in varying amounts. Pectin encourages fruit juices to jell. But it needs sugar and an acid to work. If jams do not have enough sugar to bond with the pectin, the jams won't jell properly. Lemon juice acidifies the fruit, which helps the pectin to bond with the sugar.

Most commercially available pectin is made from apples or citrus pith. You can make jam with less sugar, but you will need a special pectin. If you skip pectin altogether, by the time you cook the fruit down to a jam consistency, it will lose its fresh taste and bright color.

Any fruit contains the most pectin just before it ripens. Once it begins to soften, the pectin starts to break down, so just-ripe fruit is the best choice for jam making.

Fruits that are high in pectin include:

- gooseberries
- black and red currants
- apples
- quince
- the skin of citrus fruits

Fruits that are low in pectin include:

- sweet and sour cherries
- grapes
- strawberries
- raspberries
- blueberries

what you'll need to make berry jam

- kitchen scale

- 2 lb (1 kg) carefully sorted berries

- 1½ lb (750 g) sugar

- one grated green or unripe apple, skin and flesh but no core

- ¼ cup (2 fl oz/60 ml) fresh lemon juice

- 5-qt (5-l) heavy-bottomed nonreactive saucepan or stockpot

- wooden spoon

- 2 small plates, chilled

- ladle

- canning jar funnel (optional)

- 4 or 5 half-pint (8 fl oz/ 250 ml) canning jars with self-sealing lids and metal-ring bands

1 weigh the berries and sugar

Weighing everything ensures that your jam will be the right sweetness and will set. If you're using strawberries, hull and slice them before weighing.

2 mix and mash

Mix the berries, sugar, grated apple, and lemon juice in the pot. It should not be more than half full or the jam will spatter. Stir with the wooden spoon until well mixed and the berries are mashed and nice and juicy.

3 bubbly boiling fruit

Bring to a boil over medium-high heat. Use the spoon to skim off the foam that rises to the top. This will keep the finished jam clean. Boil for 15 minutes. Stir frequently until you feel the fruit start to stick to the pot bottom, and then stir constantly.

4 test your jam

When the jam is very thick, drop a small amount onto a chilled plate. If the jam is thick and the juices don't run, it's ready. If not, cook for 5 minutes longer and check again. Repeat if necessary. Most berry jams will jell in about 15 minutes. Juicy berries might take a little longer.

5 fill your jam jars

Ladle the hot jam into the clean jars. Seal with the lids and ring bands. Turn the jars upside down and let cool completely. Turn the jars right side up and press the center of each lid. If it remains depressed, store the jars in a cool place for up to 1 year. If not, keep it in the refrigerator and eat within 3 weeks.

These delicious jammy bars get most of their sweetness from the jam filling. The crumbly pastry, with its oatmeal and nut crunch, is reminiscent of a crumble topping. If you like your bars sweeter, add an additional ½ cup (5 oz/155 g) jam. Let the kids mix the crumbly dough and assemble the bars. After making them, they will likely insist on bringing them to school in their lunchbox—a healthy and yummy snack.

oatmeal jammy bars

1½ cups (7½ oz/235 g) all-purpose (plain) flour

½ cup (3½ oz/105 g) firmly packed golden brown sugar

1 teaspoon kosher salt

1 teaspoon baking powder

¼ teaspoon baking soda (bicarbonate of soda)

¾ cup (6 oz/185 g) cold unsalted butter, cut into cubes

1¼ cups (3¾ oz/115 g) old-fashioned rolled oats

¼ cup (1 oz/30 g) ground pecans or almonds (optional)

½ cup (5 oz/155 g) berry jam, homemade (page 102) or store-bought

makes 10 bars

Preheat the oven to 350°F (180°C). Butter a 9-inch (23-cm) square baking pan or dish.

In a large bowl, stir together the flour, sugar, salt, baking powder, and baking soda, using your hands to combine thoroughly. Scatter the butter pieces over the flour mixture and cut in the butter with a pastry cutter or two kitchen knives until the mixture is moist and crumbly. Add the oats and nuts, if using, and toss to mix evenly.

Press two-thirds of the dough into the bottom of the prepared pan. Spread the jam evenly over the top. Crumble the remaining dough evenly over the top, and press down lightly.

Bake until the top is golden brown, 35–40 minutes. Let cool completely on a rack, and then cut into bars.

Winter delivers bushels of inexpensive tropical fruits to our shores. It's the only time that mangoes or papayas seem like a bargain. I dice the fruits and freeze them for future smoothies. My daughters like their smoothies made with ice and no yogurt—but I like mine with yogurt and no ice.

tropical smoothies

1 cup (5 oz/155 g) *each* **diced mango, diced papaya, and pineapple chunks**

4 cups (32 fl oz/1 l) assorted tropical fruit juices such as mango, tangerine, orange, passionfruit, pineapple, papaya, or coconut

3 ripe bananas, peeled and halved

1½ cups (12 oz/375 g) plain or vanilla yogurt

crushed ice

lime wedges for garnish

makes 6 smoothies

If you or your kids like frozen smoothies, have the juices well chilled, freeze the diced fruit, and have the crushed ice on hand.

To make each smoothie, in a bowl, stir together the diced mango, papaya, and pineapple. Select 1 or 2 juices for a total of ⅔ cup (5 fl oz/160 ml), and pour into a blender. Add ½ banana; ½ cup (3 oz/90 g) mixed diced fruit; ¼ cup (2 oz/60 g) yogurt; and a handful of ice. Process until smooth, pour into a tall glass, and garnish with a lime wedge for squeezing in a little brightness before sipping.

get creative

Here are three great combinations:

- *⅓ cup (3 fl oz/80 ml) each passion fruit and tangerine juice, ½ banana, and ½ cup (3 oz/90 g) diced mango.*

- *⅓ cup (3 fl oz/80 ml) each pineapple and coconut juice, ½ banana, ¼ cup (1½ oz/45 g) diced pineapple, and ¼ cup (2 oz/60 g) plain or vanilla yogurt.*

- *⅓ cup (3 fl oz/80 ml) each papaya and tangerine juice, ¼ cup (1½ oz/45 g) each diced mango and papaya, and ½ cup (3 oz/90 g) diced pineapple.*

In our yard, we have several heirloom apple trees—whose names I've forgotten—that produce fruit perfect for making this sauce. My younger daughter eats cups of it for lunch. It is also a great accompaniment to pork (page 215). If your family likes tart apple sauce, use less sugar—or none at all.

chunky applesauce

Peel, quarter, and core each apple, and then cut into chunks. You should have about 4 cups (1 lb/500 g) diced apples. Place in a saucepan, add the sugar, ¼ cup (2 fl oz/60 ml) water, lemon juice, and salt, and stir well. Bring to a boil over medium-high heat, reduce the heat to low, cover, and simmer until tender, about 30 minutes. If the apples begin to dry out before they are ready, add a little more water.

Uncover the pan and mash the apples lightly with a wooden spoon or a silicone spatula. Continue to cook for 5 minutes longer to evaporate some of the excess moisture. The applesauce should be thick. Remove from the heat and serve warm or chilled.

get creative

You can use a mix of 2 pears and 2 apples, or use all pears. You can also scent the sauce with a pinch of ground cinnamon, or add ¼ cup (1 oz/30 g) fresh cranberries and increase the sugar to 1 cup (8 oz/250 g) to balance the tartness. For a savory sauce, which pairs well with pork, add ½ teaspoon chopped fresh thyme and season to taste with salt and pepper.

4 Fuji or Braeburn apples

¼ cup (2 oz/60 g) sugar

2 teaspoons fresh lemon juice

pinch of kosher salt

serves 4–6

Lemonade is the perfect thirst quencher during our hot summer. But by the time summer rolls around, we have long ago picked the last of our lemons. So every winter, at least twice a month, my daughters and I pick as many lemons as we possibly can, zest and juice them, and then freeze our labor for summertime use.

summertime lemonade

To make the simple syrup, in a small saucepan, combine the water and sugar, stir to combine, and bring to a boil over medium-high heat. Reduce the heat to medium and simmer for 5 minutes. Pour into a heatproof container, let cool completely, and refrigerate until well chilled. You should have 1¼–1½ cups (10–12 fl oz/310–375 ml). It will keep indefinitely.

To make the lemonade, pour the lemon juice into a 2½-qt (2.5-l) pitcher. Add the simple syrup to taste. If you are using a sweet lemon, such as a Meyer, you will need less syrup. Add the water, stir to blend, and then add ice. Pour into tall glasses, garnish with the lemon slices, and serve right away.

for the simple syrup

1 cup (8 fl oz/250 ml) water

1 cup (8 oz/250 g) sugar

1 cup (8 fl oz/250 ml) fresh lemon juice

4 cups (32 fl oz/1 l) cold water

ice cubes

1 lemon, thinly sliced and slices seeded

serves 6

We decided to plant fruit trees instead of a lawn, which would just suck water and give nothing back. We figured that once the trees were established, they would need very little water and would yield both fruit and shade from the hot summer sun. The first year we picked only two plums, which we paraded about with great ceremony. The next year we had enough peaches and apples to make some pies and a few jars of jam. But my great hope, the Morello cherry tree, remained barren.

Three years passed. Then in late spring, I noticed the nubs of hundreds of cherries buried amid the leaves. They swelled with each passing week, and I began to anticipate a July harvest. Abruptly, the leaves started to fall off the tree, a few at first and then great clumps. When harvest was about a week away, my father-in-law commented, "Nice cherries. What happened to the leaves?" I didn't know. Suddenly, I began to fear the tree would die, so I started to pick the almost-ripe cherries, about a handful a day, and pitted and froze them. They tasted tart at the center but sweet at first bite, with a bitter almond finish. I ended up with eight quarts (liters) that year, enough for a pie and a few batches of turnovers. The flavor of the cherries was so haunting and pure, I couldn't wait for the next harvest.

Each new crop of cherries brings with it an immense plan of possibilities. Think warm cherry pie, cherry–chocolate chunk ice cream, and cherry jam. Whether eaten out of hand or quick-cooked into a compote to crown yogurt, cherries top the favorite fruit list of most kids and adults alike.

Cherries, especially sour cherries, have a hint of almond flavor, which intensifies when you pair them with the real thing. My daughters have become proficient at filling and sealing big batches of these turnovers for large breakfast parties. We also like to serve them as individual "hand pies" at barbecues.

toasty almond–cherry turnovers

⅓ recipe **Quick Puff Pastry (page 279)**, or I sheet store-bought all-butter frozen puff pastry, II by I7 inches (28 by 43 cm), thawed according to package directions

2 tablespoons ground almonds

2 tablespoons confectioners' (icing) sugar

I cup pitted and stemmed (6 oz/185 g) sour or Bing cherries, fresh, thawed frozen, or drained canned

½ cup (4 oz/125 g) plus 2 tablespoons granulated sugar

I tablespoon all-purpose (plain) flour

I large egg white, lightly beaten

¼ cup (I oz/30 g) sliced (flaked) almonds

makes 6 turnovers

Line a baking sheet with parchment (baking) paper. On a floured work surface roll out the pastry into an 18-by-12 inch (45-by-30-cm) rectangle, about ⅛ inch (3 mm) thick. Cut the rectangle into six 6-inch (15-cm) squares. In a small bowl, stir together the ground almonds and the confectioners' sugar. In a medium bowl, stir together the cherries, ½ cup of the granulated sugar, and the flour.

Place 2 teaspoons of the almond mixture in the center of each square. Divide the cherry mixture evenly among the squares, placing it on the almond mixture. Brush 2 contiguous sides of each square lightly with egg white and fold in half to form a triangle. Crimp the edges with fork tines to seal. Place the pastries on the prepared pan, spacing them 1½ inches (4 cm) apart. Refrigerate for 30 minutes. (At this point, the turnovers can be well wrapped and frozen for up to 3 months and then topped and baked directly from the freezer, increasing the baking time in the hot oven to 30 minutes.)

Preheat the oven to 425°F (220°C). Recrimp the edges of each triangle with the fork. Brush the tops lightly with egg white. Sprinkle evenly with sliced almonds and then with the 2 tablespoons granulated sugar. Using a sharp knife, cut 2 small vents in the top of each triangle.

Bake for 20 minutes. Reduce the heat to 350°F (180°C) and continue to bake until puffed and golden, 10 to 15 minutes longer. Let cool on the pan on a rack. Serve warm.

Blueberry pie and vanilla ice cream is a match made in heaven—one our family looks forward to every summer. When it is time to make the pie, I ready the pastry while the kids pick over the berries, discarding the funky ones, and then toss them with sugar. I roll out the dough and the kids cut the strips and place them on the pie. We get some pretty crazy designs, but they are all beautiful when the pies are pulled from the oven.

blueberry pie

On a lightly floured work surface, roll out half of the pastry into a 12-inch (30-cm) round about ⅛ inch (3 mm) thick. Loosely roll the pastry around the rolling pin, center it over a 9-inch pie pan, then unroll and fit it into the dish, pressing it against the bottom and sides. Trim the overhang to about 1 inch (2.5 cm).

In a bowl, toss together the blueberries, lemon juice, and vanilla. Add the ½ cup sugar, the flour, and the salt, and toss again to coat the berries evenly. Pour the blueberries into the pie shell, and dot the filling with the butter.

To make the lattice top, roll out the dough into a round the same size as the bottom crust, and cut into strips ½ inch (12 mm) wide. Place the longest strip across the center of the pie, and place about half of the shorter strips on either side, spacing them evenly, ¼ inch (6 mm) apart. Rotate the pie 90 degrees. Place the remaining strips perpendicular to the first layer of dough strips, spacing them evenly. Trim any long strips even with the bottom crust, then fold the bottom crust over the ends of the strips and crimp with your fingers or fork tines. Refrigerate for 30 minutes.

Preheat the oven to 400°F (200°C). Brush the top crust with the milk and sprinkle with the 1 tablespoon sugar. Bake until the fruit is bubbling and the crust is golden, 50–60 minutes. Let cool on a rack. Serve with a big scoop of ice cream.

double recipe Homemade Pastry Dough (page 278), or 2 store-bought pie pastry rounds for a 9-inch (23-cm) pie

4 cups (1 lb/500 g) fresh or frozen blueberries

1 tablespoon lemon juice

½ teaspoon pure vanilla extract

½ cup (4 oz/125 g) sugar plus 1 tablespoon

3 tablespoons all-purpose (plain) flour

pinch of kosher salt

4 tablespoons (2 oz/60 g) cold unsalted butter, cut into small chunks

2 tablespoons whole milk

The Best Vanilla Ice Cream (page 71) for serving

makes one 9-inch (23-cm) pie

Rather than throw away overripe bananas, I peel and freeze them for making these muffins for school snacks. The recipe makes 12 regular or 24 mini muffins, the latter a good size for small children—though I do see a lot of teachers hanging around their classrooms on the days I bring them in.

banana–brown sugar muffins

1 cup (4 oz/125 g) whole wheat (wholemeal) pastry flour or graham flour

1 cup (5 oz/155 g) all-purpose (plain) flour

1 teaspoon baking soda (bicarbonate of soda)

¼ teaspoon kosher salt

2 cups (12 oz/375 g) smashed bananas (about 5 medium bananas)

¼ cup (2 fl oz/60 ml) whole milk

¾ cup (6 oz/185 g) firmly packed brown sugar

½ cup (4 oz/125 g) unsalted butter, at room temperature

2 large eggs

1 teaspoon pure vanilla extract

makes 12 standard muffins or 24 mini muffins

Preheat the oven to 350°F (180°C). Butter 12 standard muffin cups or 24 miniature muffin cups, then flour them, tapping out the excess.

In a small bowl, stir together the flours, baking soda, and salt. In another bowl, whisk together the bananas and milk.

In the bowl of a stand mixer, using the paddle attachment, beat together the brown sugar and butter on medium-high speed until light and fluffy. Stop the mixer and scrape down the sides of the bowl. Add the eggs, one at a time, beating well after each addition. On low speed, stir in the vanilla and the banana mixture, then stir in the flour mixture just until thoroughly incorporated. Spoon the batter into the prepared muffin cups, filling them two-thirds full.

Bake until the tops are golden and spring back when lightly pressed with a fingertip, 17–20 minutes for standard muffins and 12–15 minutes for the mini muffins. Let cool for 5 minutes in the pan, then turn out onto a rack. Serve warm or at room temperature.

get creative

You can top these delicious muffins with the same crumble topping used in the Apricot Crumble (page 120), or spice up the recipe by adding ½ teaspoon ground cinnamon to the flour mixture. These are also great with a handful of chopped, toasted pecans or walnuts or dried currants added to the batter just before spooning it into the pans.

Plums are particularly luscious in this preparation because the tannins in their skins, which are similar to the tannins in grape skins, add a nice tartness to the baking juices. The pigments in the skins also turn the juices a glorious purple. If the plum halves are large, add some extra brown sugar.

roasted plums with cream

Preheat the oven to 400°F (200°C). Butter a 9-by-7-inch (23-by-18-cm) or similar-sized baking dish. Place the plums, cut side up, in the prepared dish and sprinkle with the brown sugar and then the salt. Dot the pit hollows with the butter.

Bake for 20 minutes. Turn the plums over and continue to bake until soft and the juices are bubbly, 15–20 minutes longer. If the juices become dry and start to burn before the plums are ready, add a little hot water, 2 tablespoons at a time, just to cover the bottom of the dish and loosen up the thickened juice.

Meanwhile, in a bowl, combine the crème fraîche, sugar, and vanilla. Whisk together until light and fluffy peaks have formed. Divide the plums, cut side up, among individual plates, and serve warm, with the fluffy crème fraîche on the side.

get creative

Fresh prune plums, such as Italian, French, or Damson, are also wonderful prepared this way. Double the number of plums if they are particularly small, and keep the rest of the ingredient measurements the same. Other stone fruits, such as peaches and nectarines, can also be baked; adjust the baking timing according to their size.

6 Santa Rosa or other medium, red, flavorful plums, halved and pitted

½ cup (3½ oz/105 g) firmly packed golden brown sugar

¼ teaspoon kosher salt

4 tablespoons (2 oz/60 g) unsalted butter, cut into bits

1 cup (8 oz/250 g) crème fraîche, homemade (page 279) or store-bought

1 tablespoon granulated sugar

¼ teaspoon pure vanilla extract

serves 4–6

Crumbles are the busy cook's pies. No messing with a crust: just plop the fruit in a baking dish and scatter a crumbly topping over it. Kids can pit the apricots, make the topping, and assemble the crumble with very little adult help. Keep it simple, or serve with a dollop of whipped cream (page 278) or scoops of vanilla ice cream (page 71).

apricot crumble

for the crumble topping

¾ cup (4 oz/125 g) all-purpose (plain) flour

¾ cup (6 oz/ 185 g) firmly packed brown sugar

½ teaspoon kosher salt

¼ teaspoon cinnamon

½ cup (4 oz/125 g) unsalted butter, at room temperature, cut into chunks

5 cups (scant 2 lb/1 kg) pitted apricots, cut into chunks

2 teaspoons fresh lemon juice

½ teaspoon pure vanilla extract

2 tablespoons all-purpose (plain) flour

⅓ cup (3 oz/90 g) granulated sugar

serves 6–8

Preheat the oven to 400°F (200°C). Butter a 9-inch (23-cm) pie dish or 9-by-7-inch (23-by-18-cm) baking dish.

To make the topping, in a bowl, stir together the flour, brown sugar, salt, and cinnamon. Scatter the butter over the flour mixture and, using a pastry cutter or two table knives, mix until the butter is evenly distributed and the mixture begins to form clumps.

In a large bowl, toss together the apricots, lemon juice, and vanilla. Add the flour and granulated sugar and toss again to coat the fruit evenly. Transfer to the prepared baking dish and sprinkle the topping evenly over the surface. Bake until the fruit is bubbling and the topping is golden, about 40 minutes. Serve warm.

get creative

The apricots can be mixed with 1 cup (4 oz/125 g) raspberries for color and a bit of zing. You can also make crumbles to follow the seasons. My first crumble of the year is strawberry-rhubarb, followed by spring apricots or cherries, summer berries, peaches, nectarines, or plums, and then late summer and fall apples, pears, or quince.

Individual cobblers are a delight to make and eat. Kids especially love desserts that are scaled to their size. Have them make the dough and choose their shapes for topping—squares, circles, stars, or crescent moons—the sky is the limit. Serve the cobblers warm with a big scoop of ice cream (page 71) for a down-home treat!

pint-sized peach cobblers

Place a rack in the lower third of the oven and preheat to 425°F (220°C). Butter 6 to 8 individual baking dishes.

In a large bowl, toss together the peaches, lemon juice, and vanilla. Add the sugar and salt and toss again to coat the fruit evenly. Divide the fruit equally among the prepared baking dishes.

To make the biscuits, in a bowl, stir together the flour, brown sugar, baking powder, baking soda, and salt. Scatter the butter over the flour mixture and cut in with a pastry blender until the dough resembles coarse cornmeal with chunks of butter the size of peas. Add the buttermilk and stir and toss with a fork just until the ingredients come together. Turn the dough out onto a lightly floured work surface and knead lightly until uniform. It will be sticky.

Pat the dough into an 8-inch (20-cm) square using more flour as needed. Cut the biscuit dough into 6 or 8 equally-sized shapes and place on top of the peaches. Brush the tops with cream.

Bake for 10 minutes. Reduce the heat to 375°F (190°C) and continue to bake until the peaches are bubbling and the crust is golden and cooked through, about 25–30 minutes. Test by inserting a knife into the center of the biscuit. It should slide out easily. Serve warm or at room temperature.

5 cups (scant 2 lb/1kg) sliced ripe peaches

2 teaspoons lemon juice

½ teaspoon pure vanilla extract

½ cup (4 oz/125 g) sugar

pinch kosher salt

for the biscuits

1 cup (5 oz/155 g) all-purpose (plain) flour

1 tablespoon brown sugar

2 teaspoons baking powder

½ teaspoon baking soda (bicarbonate of soda)

¼ teaspoon kosher salt

4 tablespoons (2 oz/60 g) cold unsalted butter, cut into chunks

¾ cup (6 fl oz/180 ml) buttermilk

2 tablespoons heavy (double) cream

makes 6–8 cobblers

Vegetables come in all shapes, sizes, and colors. It's curious to see which ones kids will have a natural affinity for and which ones will be consumed only under protest.

vegetables & herbs

An ear of sweet corn, a freshly dug potato, a cucumber clipped from a twisting vine—these are vegetables that will make you smile. They will also get you into the kitchen frying up crisp corn fritters, whipping creamy mashed potatoes, and packing bread and butter pickles into jars. Vegetables add tremendous texture and flavor to the dinner table, and pass along lots of vitamins, minerals, and fiber. Not surprisingly, any vegetable tastes best at the height of its season. Eat as much of it as you can while it is abundant and then bid it farewell for another year and move on to the season's next harvest. The luckiest eaters have a garden planted with their favorites, but if you don't, head to your local farmers' market for the best your area has to offer.

For some reason, vegetables get a bad rap. But if you've ever bitten into a ripe tomato plucked off the vine, eaten a freshly shucked pea, or nibbled on just-picked tender lettuce, then you know their reputation is ill-deserved.

seasons of plenty

HERBS

Adding herbs is an easy way to boost the flavor of any dish. How and when to use an herb depends or whether it's tender or woody stemmed. Tender-stemmed herbs, such as basil, mint, tarragon, cilantro (fresh coriander), chives, and parsley, wilt easily. They are often used raw, sprinkled on top of a dish just before serving, or tossed into salads. Cooking discolors them and destroys their delicate flavors. Oregano, marjoram, and sage are halfway between tender and woody. They have intense flavors that can be used raw or cooked in meat, fish, or vegetable dishes. Thyme and rosemary have woody stems. Their leaves don't wilt if left at room temperature, though they sometimes discolor. These are used for marinades and are great for seasoning roasts, fish, poultry, grilled vegetables, soups, and stews.

Nature has efficiently adapted vegetables and herbs to their season, much like we adapt to the warmth of summer with cotton shirts and the chill of winter with wool coats. In summertime, vegetables are thin-skinned, tender, and perishable. They require little if any cooking. Thick-skinned root vegetables, sturdy greens, and woody herbs reign during the winter. They store well and stand up to simmering and roasting.

In summer, when corn hits the market, everyone at our house gorges themselves on it until we can't bear the thought of eating another ear. In fact, each time a new vegetable ripens we do the same thing: we eat it like we can't get enough. We also cheer at the bounty of fresh herbs in the garden and use them with abandon. As the weeks pass, we become less exuberant and openly hope that new vegetables will appear. We get lazy with herbs, too, and start taking them for granted.

Then the cycle repeats with whatever is harvested next. Each vegetable and herb has its time and place on our table. Once they are no longer in the garden or at the farmers' market, they disappear from our meals. That way we are sure to eagerly await their appearance when their season returns.

a spring pea tale

Each spring as the weather warms, my younger daughter starts to bug me about peas. Not just any peas, but the tiny, sweet *petit pois* that come from our friend Nancy's farm in Healdsburg, California. She sells her glorious peas at the local farmers' market and is a legend among the many families that patronize her organically-grown vegetables and fruits. For some reason, her wares seem to have more sweetness and intensity than other farmers'. One day I asked my daughters why they think it's so, and they replied, "Because Nancy grows everything with love."

SPRING VEGETABLES

leeks
garlic
shallots
onions
new potatoes
fava (broad) beans
peas
fennel
asparagus
artichokes
mushrooms
snap beans
arugula (rocket)

FALL VEGETABLES

fresh shelling beans
hard squashes
potatoes
chard and hardy greens
leeks
broccoli
cauliflower
carrots
turnips
beets
celery
celeriac
sunchokes
savoy spinach
mushrooms

SUMMER VEGETABLES

delicate lettuces
tomatoes
green beans
summer squashes
tomatoes
eggplants (aubergines)
corn
peppers (capsicum) and chiles
carrots
baby root vegetables
beets
broccoli

WINTER VEGETABLES

cabbage
chard
kale
chicories
bitter greens
broccoli rabe
bok choy
watercress
hard squashes
root vegetables
potatoes
Brussels sprouts

Sweet ears of yellow corn, juicy red tomatoes, bright orange pumpkins, deep purple eggplant, tender green zucchini—vegetables come in a wide array of shapes, sizes, and irresistable colors.

shopping local

For the best flavor and texture, buy locally grown seasonal vegetables whenever possible. A farmers' market is the ideal place to do that. Even in winter, you may be able to find root vegetables and hard squashes grown no farther than a few counties away. When shopping at a supermarket, select whatever looks vibrant and seems seasonal. In other words, if they don't make sense, like winter squash in June and ears of corn in January, don't buy them. It means they are from another hemisphere. Tomatoes from outside your local growing area will never be as flavorful as locally harvested tomatoes, and you will pay double the price for their inferior taste. Some stores post signs indicating the origin of their produce. If you are not sure, ask a store worker.

shopping organic

How vegetables are grown should also play a part in deciding what to buy. Organic vegetables, which have been grown without the use of synthetic pesticides, herbicides, fungicides, or fertilizers, are the best choice. Vegetables cultivated without the use of synthetic pesticides, herbicides, and fungicides but with continued use of synthetic fertilizers are the next best choice. These are often announced with a sign declaring "No Spraying" or "Pesticide Free." And if you can't buy either of these, try to avoid vegetables that have high pesticide residue (see the listing to the left).

shopping for the best

Vegetables are divided into three main types: fruiting, leafy, and root. Vegetables that fruit stop ripening once they are picked. These are any vegetable cut from the leafy greenery of a plant, such as squashes, green beans, peppers (capsicums), eggplants (aubergines), and peas. At the moment they are picked, fruiting vegetables are sweet with natural sugars and their vitamin content is at its peak, but they deteriorate quickly. Their skins should be smooth, shiny, and uniformly firm, and any visible stem should be fresh looking, not withered or blackened.

Leafy greens, like fruiting vegetables, also lose their vibrancy soon after cutting, so they should be washed, spun dry, and chilled in a sealed plastic bag as soon as possible after purchase. Try to consume the most delicate greens, like lettuce, within a day or two. Hardier specimens, like chard and kale, will last for up to a week. Before you buy, check for any discoloration, slimy leaves, evidence of too many hungry insects, or a funky odor. Packaged greens are packed with carbon dioxide to extend their shelf life for up to a week. To revive wilted greens, dip them in warm water, shake off the excess, and chill in a sealed bag for a couple of hours.

Root vegetables, which include bulb vegetables like onions, are still alive when they come to market. Have you ever seen sprouting potatoes, onions, or garlic? If you planted them, they would continue to grow. The freshest root vegetables—whether carrots, beets, turnips, or rutabagas—are the ones with their tops still intact. Once the tops start to wilt, farmers or grocers usually trim them off, so you can no longer tell how long ago they were harvested. However, lopping them off dramatically increases the vegetable's shelf life because the root can stop sending energy to the tops to sustain them. That's why most root vegetables come with clipped tops. If you do find beets or turnips with lovely, fresh greens, you can sauté them in garlic and olive oil for an extra treat alongside your root vegetable dish. Choose root vegetables that feel firm and are heavy for their size. Look for firm onions with shiny papery skins, garlic that is firm and plump, and both onions and garlic free of sprouts.

your own vegetable and herb garden

When you have fresh herbs, greens, and vegetables an arm's length away, it changes the way you think about meals. Rather than a trip to the market, you can just grab your scissors, cut a few herb sprigs, and instantly add the scent of rosemary and thyme to grilled meats or roasted veggies. You can add thick slices of just-picked tomatoes to your burgers, and the lettuce in your salad will pop with freshness when you bite into it.

A garden that provides you with food not only keeps your table laden with good flavors but also sustains your soul and keeps you in touch with the natural rhythm of the seasons.

our favorite garden vegetables and herbs

vegetables

These hardy plants are easy to grow and do well in pots or a garden plot:

- red, gold, and chiogga beets
- straight and round carrots
- French breakfast radishes
- Japanese eggplant (aubergines)
- sweet 100, sungold, early girl, and beefsteak tomatoes
- bush pickles
- sweet bell peppers (capsicums)
- poblano and Anaheim chiles

greens

Plant a row or a large pot with a mix of lettuces and greens.

- little gem lettuces
- bloomsdale spinach
- frisée, radicchio, or other chicories
- rainbow Swiss chard

herbs

Herbs can be planted alone or in clusters. For a nice mix of color and texture, plant 2–3 varieties of the same herb or 2–3 different herbs in one pot or garden corner.

- marjoram and oregano
- Thai, Genovese, and opal basil
- lemon, silver, and English thyme
- tarragon, chervil, and chives
- haifa, trailing, and blue spires rosemary

what you'll need for your garden

- a variety of herb and vegetable seedlings
- a small garden plot with prepared soil or various-sized pots
- pebbles or pot shards for drainage
- soil for pots
- watering can or hose
- trowel
- plant markers

1 plan ahead

Find out what grows best in your region, then decide on the herbs, vegetables, and greens that the whole family likes to eat and that you want to plant.

2 a pot or a plot?

Decide whether you want to use pots or a garden plot. Most herbs and lettuces and some vegetables can be grown in pots. If you use pots, you can bring herbs and lettuces indoors in winter, for a year-round harvest. If you use a garden plot, make sure it has good drainage.

3 find a spot

Whether you decide on a pot or a plot, make sure you select a good, sunny spot. Plants that fruit need a site with at least 6 hours of sunlight daily. Greens can handle partial shade.

4 get your pots ready

If you are using pots, put the pebbles or pot shards around the hole in the bottom to promote good drainage. Fill the pot nearly full with good, rich potting soil.

5 get dirty

Give the soil a good watering before planting. Line up the seedlings in their little pots in the place you want to plant them. Press the pot into the soil to mark the spot. Using the trowel, make a hole in the soil just big enough for the plant.

6 plant it

Give the seedlings a drink of water before you begin transplanting them, then gently remove from the container. Carefully spread out the clumped roots, put in the ground or pot, and lightly press the dirt around the base of the plant. Give them a little more water.

7 watch it grow!

Label your plants with plant markers so you don't forget what you planted where, then water them and wish them luck. After that, water as needed and keep up on the weeds.

This salad shows off the bright flavor of fresh greens and fragrant herbs. Mix different kinds of greens—like bitter curly endive (chicory) and radicchio, spicy watercress and arugula (rocket), and mild butter (Boston) lettuce and baby spinach. If using lettuces from your garden, show the kids how to harvest them, then have them rinse and dry the greens and the herbs and toss the salad together.

herbed garden salad with goat cheese

6 cups (6 oz/185 g) mixed salad greens

1 cup (1 oz/30 g) mixed fresh herb leaves such as tarragon, flat-leaf parsley, dill, chervil, and chives, in any combination

extra-virgin olive oil

kosher salt and freshly ground pepper

¼ teaspoon sugar

white wine vinegar

½ lb (250 g) fresh goat cheese, crumbled

serves 6–8

In a large bowl, combine the greens and herbs. Drizzle with just enough oil to coat lightly and then toss. Season with salt and pepper and the sugar, and then toss the greens again and taste.

Drizzle with 1–2 teaspoons vinegar and toss. Taste for tanginess and seasoning and adjust with salt, pepper, and vinegar as needed.

Sprinkle the goat cheese over the top and serve right away.

get creative

Make a season of salads:

In spring, add sliced blanched asparagus, diced artichoke hearts, or fava (broad) beans with cubed pecorino.

In summer, toss in fresh corn kernels, ripe cherry tomatoes or diced heirloom tomatoes, and cucumber slices.

In fall, add apple, pear, or Fuyu persimmon slices, or pomegranate seeds.

In winter, tangerine, grapefruit, or blood orange sections are good additions. Crushed or whole toasted almonds, pine nuts, or pecans add crunch, while a blue-veined cheese, such as Gorgonzola, or shards of a salty, nutty hard cheese, like pecorino or Parmigiano-Reggiano, can replace the mild goat cheese.

These sweet-and-sour pickles are completely addictive, whether served alongside burgers at a summertime barbecue or chopped and added to homemade tartar sauce. Older kids can help cut the cucumbers and onions with adult supervision. Smaller children can help pack the pickles in the jar after they have cooled.

bread-n-butter pickles

Have ready a 1-qt (1-l) canning jar or other glass jar with a lid. Slice the cucumber about ⅛ inch (3 mm) thick; you should have about 4 cups. In a stainless steel or other nonreactive heatproof bowl, combine the cucumber and onion.

In a small nonreactive saucepan, combine the vinegar, sugar, salt, celery and mustard seeds, and bay leaves, and bring to a boil over high heat, stirring to dissolve the sugar and salt. Immediately pour the vinegar mixture over the cucumber and onion slices. Let cool to room temperature, and then pack the vegetables and liquid into the jar, discarding any excess liquid. Cover tightly and refrigerate. The pickles will keep for up to 1 month.

get creative

To make pickles that can be stored at room temperature, pack the pickles and onions in a clean, dry, sterilized 1-qt (1-l) canning jar and ladle in the hot pickling liquid to within ½ inch (12 mm) of the rim. Top with a sterilized lid, and seal tightly with a screw band. Process in a hot-water bath for 10 minutes. Turn the jars upside down and let cool completely. Turn the jars right side up and press the center of each lid. If it remains depressed, store the jars in a cool, dark place for up to 1 year. If not, keep it in the refrigerator and eat within 1 month.

1 English (hothouse) cucumber or 6 pickling cucumbers (about 1 lb/ 500 g)

1 white onion, thinly sliced

2 cups (16 fl oz/500 ml) white wine vinegar

¾ cup (6 oz/185 g) sugar

¼ cup (1½ oz/45 g) kosher salt

1 teaspoon celery seeds

1 teaspoon mustard seeds

2 bay leaves

makes 1 qt (1 l)

I have eaten minestrone for as long as I can remember. My great-grandmother Nana DiGregorio from Italy made the best. She piled it full of vegetables from her garden in summer and added her flavorful home-canned tomatoes to the broth in winter. Happiness was sitting down to a bowl of soup as big as my head and soaking bread in the broth until it was gone. Only then would I eat the spoonfuls of vegetables left stranded in the bottom of the bowl. If I was lucky I would find a square of chewy, partially melted Parmesan rind tucked under the vegetables. It was like finding the golden ticket.

The first time I made minestrone for my kids, they initially turned up their noses. I was stunned. I thought they would love it as much as I had as a child. So I told them the story about the soup my Nana made and how I would visit her just so I could eat it. They thought about what I said and took a taste of the soup I had made with so much love and happy memories. They took another bite. Soon they were digging in with gusto and vying for more bread. My older daughter took the leftovers to school the next day and told her friends the story of the minestrone. My soup has become a legend at school, and we have added another favorite dish to the family repertoire.

Many of my friends use my simple minestrone recipe as a clearinghouse for fresh vegetables that rapidly accumulate in their vegetable crispers and countertop baskets. Fresh peas, potatoes, summer squash, corn, green beans, or any of your favorite vegetables can be added to make your own family brand of minestrone.

I love this vegetarian minestrone, and so does everyone in my family. I often serve it when guests are invited for a casual supper, rounding out the menu with crusty bread and a green salad. Save the rinds from Parmesan cheese, freeze them, and add a square to the soup pot. It will add richness and complexity to the broth. For additional flavor, you can also use a light vegetable broth in place of the water.

veggie minestrone

extra-virgin olive oil

2 large cloves garlic

2 carrots, diced

1 small onion, diced

1 stalk celery, thinly sliced

kosher salt and freshly ground pepper

1 cup (6 oz/185 g) diced fresh or canned tomatoes with their juice

1 bay leaf

2 large fresh sage leaves

2 cups (15 oz/425 g) drained canned or home-cooked (page 281) cannellini beans

2 cups (6 oz/185 g) packed shredded kale or chard

1 cup (4 oz/125 g) tubettini or other small dried pasta shape

grated Parmesan cheese for garnish

serves 8–10

Heat a large soup pot over medium-high heat. Add 1 tablespoon oil and the garlic and sauté until the garlic is toasted and the oil is fragrant, about 1 minute. Add the carrot, onion, and celery and cook, stirring often, until the vegetables start to soften and brown, 3–4 minutes. Season with salt and pepper.

Add the tomatoes, bay, sage, a 2-inch (5-cm) Parmesan cheese rind (if desired, see note above), and enough water to cover the vegetables by 2 inches (5 cm) and simmer, uncovered, for 30 minutes. Add the beans and kale and continue to simmer for 20–30 minutes. Season to taste with salt and pepper.

Just before the soup is ready, bring a saucepan three-fourths full of salted water to a boil, add the pasta, stir well, and cook until al dente, according to package directions. Drain well and divide among warmed soup bowls. Ladle the soup over the pasta, drizzle with oil, sprinkle generously with the grated cheese, and serve.

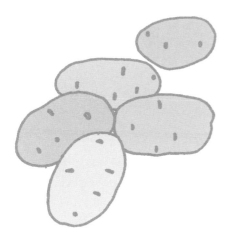

The last time I made these potatoes, the kids tried to eat them by dipping their fingers into the bowl and scooping up huge mounds. I had to slap them gently away or risk having no potatoes to serve for dinner. Be sure to use potatoes that fall halfway between starchy and waxy and have a buttery flavor.

creamiest mashed potatoes

kosher salt

4 large Yukon gold or Yellow Finn potatoes, about 2 lb (1 kg) total weight, peeled and quartered

3 large cloves garlic (optional)

½ cup (4 fl oz/125 ml) whole milk

½ cup (4 fl oz/125 ml) heavy (double) cream

2 tablespoons unsalted butter

pinch of freshly grated nutmeg (optional)

serves 6–8

Fill a saucepan about three-fourths full of water, add 2 tablespoons salt, and then the potatoes and garlic, if using. Bring to a boil, reduce the heat to a simmer, and cook, uncovered, until the potatoes easily slide off the blade of a knife when poked, about 30 minutes. Drain into a colander in the sink.

Pass the hot potatoes through a ricer into a large bowl. The potatoes can also be placed in a large bowl and mashed with a potato masher or a large fork, but they will be slightly lumpier in texture. Cover the bowl with a dish towel to keep warm.

In a small saucepan, combine the milk, cream, and butter, and bring to just below a boil over medium heat. Immediately remove from the heat. Gradually add the milk mixture to the potatoes while stirring with a fork. The potatoes should be smooth and thick. Beat the potatoes a few times with a large spoon to smooth them out. Add the nutmeg, if using, season to taste with salt, and serve right away.

get creative

Use sour cream or crème fraîche instead of the cream for a tangier dish. Stir in 1 tablespoon chopped fresh chives or dill just before serving. You can also cook and mash celery root (celeriac), parsnips, or other root vegetables separately and then mix them with the potatoes for added texture and flavor.

Caramelizing vegetables in a hot oven brings out their natural sweetness. Asparagus, Brussels sprouts, and broccoli are given a whole new delicious life using this simple method. Trim the asparagus, cut the sprouts in half, and adjust the cooking time as needed.

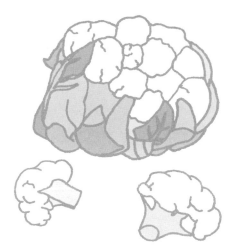

roasted cauliflower

Preheat the oven to 425°F (220°C). Cut off the green outer leaves from the cauliflower, and then cut the cauliflower in half. Cut out the core. Cut the cauliflower crosswise into slices ½ inch (12 mm) thick.

Drizzle a rimmed baking sheet with the oil and sprinkle evenly with the salt. Arrange the cauliflower in a single layer on top, and then flip the cauliflower over to coat the second sides with oil and salt.

Roast until golden on the first sides, about 15 minutes. Turn the slices over and continue to roast until golden on the second sides until tender, 10–15 minutes longer. Transfer to a platter, sprinkle with the pepper flakes, and serve at once.

1 head cauliflower, about 1½ lb (750 g)

3 tablespoons extra-virgin olive oil

1 teaspoon sea salt

¼ teaspoon red pepper flakes (optional)

serves 4–6

Dressing grilled vegetables with nothing more than really good extra-virgin olive oil and a sprinkle of some nice sea salt allows the subtle, individual flavor of each vegetable to shine through. If you have a favorite vegetable, add it to the mix. I like to grill asparagus, sliced potatoes, and baby leeks in spring when they are at their best.

grilled vegetable antipasto

Trim the eggplants, zucchini, and yellow squash, slice lengthwise ¼ inch (6 mm) thick, and place in a large bowl. Seed and stem the peppers, trim away the ribs, and cut lengthwise into strips about 1 inch (2.5 cm) wide. Add to the bowl. Trim off the stems from the mushrooms and, using a small spoon, scrape out and discard the black gills. Quarter the caps and add to the bowl. Peel and trim the red onions, slice them into thick wedges, and add to the bowl.

Drizzle the vegetables with ¼ cup (2 fl oz/60 ml) oil, add the thyme, and season with salt and pepper. Toss to coat the vegetables evenly. Let stand for 15–20 minutes to allow the vegetables to release some of their juices. Toss again just before grilling.

Meanwhile, prepare a medium-hot fire in a charcoal or gas grill. Make sure the grill rack is clean, then oil it and let the oil burn off for about 5 minutes.

Working in batches, place the vegetables on the grill rack and grill, turning once, until golden and tender, 2–3 minutes on each side. (If you are preparing the optional red onion vinaigrette, grill the onion slices alongside the vegetables.) Transfer to a platter. When all of the vegetables are cooked, drizzle with oil or with the red onion vinaigrette and serve.

2 small Japanese eggplants (aubergines)

1 small zucchini (courgette)

1 small yellow squash

1 small red bell pepper (capsicum)

1 small yellow bell pepper (capsicum)

2 large portobello mushrooms

2 red onions

extra-virgin olive oil

2 teaspoons chopped fresh thyme

sea salt and freshly ground pepper

vegetable oil for grill rack

Grilled Red Onion Vinaigrette (page 280; optional)

serves 4–6

The amazing variety of tomatoes available in summer—from cherry to heirloom to beefsteak and more—makes this salad a kaleidoscope of color. Put your kids to work picking the basil leaves from their stems. They will also be happy to arrange the colorful tomato slices and wedges on a platter, their very own creation of edible art.

tomato-mozzarella salad with pesto

for the pesto

kosher salt and freshly ground pepper

1 cup (1½ oz/45 g) packed fresh basil leaves

2 tablespoons pine nuts, lightly toasted

1 clove garlic

¼ cup (2 fl oz/60 ml) extra-virgin olive oil

1 lb (500 g) mixed heirloom tomatoes, in a variety of colors and sizes

1 cup (6 oz/185 g) halved assorted cherry tomatoes

extra-virgin olive oil

sea salt and freshly ground black pepper

½ lb (250 g) fresh mozzarella cheese, in large and/or small balls

serves 4–6

To make the pesto, in a saucepan, bring 4 cups (32 fl oz/1 l) water to a boil, and add 2 tablespoons salt. Add the basil leaves and boil for 30 seconds. Drain in a sieve and place under cold running water to cool. Squeeze the leaves to remove the excess water and place in a food processor. (Blanching the leaves helps them keep their bright green color.) Add the pine nuts and garlic and process until finely chopped. Season with ¼ teaspoon salt and a few grinds of pepper. With the machine running, drizzle in the oil and process to a fine paste. Transfer to a bowl and season with salt and pepper. If not using within 2 hours, press a piece of plastic wrap against the surface of the pesto.

Core and slice the heirloom tomatoes ¼ inch (6 mm) thick. Cut smaller tomatoes into wedges. In a bowl, toss all the tomatoes with 2 tablespoons oil, and season with salt and pepper. Arrange on a plate.

Slice large mozzarella balls ¼ inch thick and slip between the tomato slices. Or, cut small balls in half and scatter over the tomatoes. Using a small spoon, place dabs of pesto on top of the tomatoes. (If the pesto is very stiff, whisk in a little oil to loosen it up.) Grind pepper over the top and serve. Pass the remaining pesto at the table.

My daughters and their friends are crazy about these puffy fritters and constantly beg me to make a batch with them. The kids can add the ingredients and stir them together, but make sure an adult takes over when it's time to fry. Make them in the summertime when corn is at its peak of flavor. The lime juice brings out the sweetness of the kernels, so have plenty of wedges on hand for serving.

corn fritters with lime

In a small bowl, stir together the corn kernels and lime juice. In a medium bowl, whisk together the egg, milk, and butter until blended. In a large bowl, stir together the flour, cornmeal, baking powder, salt, and cayenne. Quickly mix the egg mixture into the flour mixture until smooth. Fold in the corn.

Pour the oil to a depth of 1 inch (2.5 cm) into a deep saucepan and heat to 375°F (180°C) on a deep-frying thermometer. Put 1 or 2 wire racks on a large rimmed baking sheet and place near the stove.

Drop the batter by heaping tablespoons into the hot oil, being careful not to crowd the pan. Fry until browned on one side, about 2 minutes. Flip the fritters over and fry until golden, puffed, and cooked through, 2–3 minutes longer. Keep the kids away from the pan to protect against burns from popping corn kernels. Using a slotted spoon, transfer to the rack to drain. Repeat until all of the batter is used up. Transfer the hot fritters to a napkin-lined basket and serve right away with the lime wedges.

get creative

For a more savory flair, dress up the batter with 1 teaspoon chopped green (spring) onion, 1 teaspoon chopped fresh cilantro (fresh coriander), and ¼ cup (1 oz/30 g) shredded Cheddar cheese, folding them in with the corn. For an even sweeter turn, dust the fritters with confectioners' sugar, but still pass plenty of lime wedges.

1½ cups (9 oz/280 g) fresh corn kernels (from about 3 ears), chopped

2 teaspoons fresh lime juice

1 large egg

½ cup (4 fl oz/125 ml) whole milk

2 tablespoons unsalted butter, melted and cooled

¾ cup (4 oz/125 g) all-purpose (plain) flour

¼ cup (1½ oz/45 g) fine-grind cornmeal

1 teaspoon baking powder

¾ teaspoon kosher salt

⅛ teaspoon cayenne

expeller-pressed canola oil for deep-frying

lime wedges for serving

makes about 24 fritters

When the parsley in our garden starts to look bushy in early July, I know it's time to make this classic Lebanese salad. Bursting with nutrients and fiber, it has a refreshing taste that is the perfect foil to the richly spiced meats and sauces of the eastern Mediterranean table.

tabbouleh

I cup (6 oz/185 g) bulgur wheat

kosher salt and freshly ground pepper

I cup (8 fl oz/250 ml) boiling water

I English (hothouse) cucumber

I large, ripe tomato

I cup (1½ oz/45 g) chopped fresh flat-leaf (Italian) parsley

¼ cup (⅓ oz/10 g) chopped fresh mint

¼ cup (¾ oz/20 g) thinly sliced green (spring) onion, including tender green tops

¼ cup (2 fl oz/60 ml) fresh lemon juice

3 tablespoons olive oil

¼ teaspoon ground allspice

serves 4–6

Place the bulgur in a heatproof bowl. Dissolve I teaspoon salt in the boiling water and pour over the bulgur. Cover tightly with plastic wrap and let stand at room temperature for 30 minutes. The bulgur will absorb the water, swell, split, and fluff.

Peel, seed, and dice the cucumber. Seed and dice the tomato. Add the cucumber, tomato, parsley, mint, green onion, lemon juice, oil, and allspice to the bulgur and stir and toss to mix well. Season to taste with salt and pepper, holding back a little on the salt. Cover and set aside at room temperature for at least I hour, or refrigerate for up to I day, to allow the flavors to marry. Taste and adjust the seasoning with salt and pepper and serve.

I used to fry the breaded eggplant on the stove top, but I found the eggplant absorbed too much oil, which destroyed its delicacy. Now I oven-fry the eggplant, which is easier, keeps its texture intact, and produces a custardy finish. Look for an eggplant that feels heavy with a shiny, smooth skin.

eggplant parmigiana

Preheat the oven to 400°F (200°C). Pour the oil onto a large rimmed baking sheet and swirl to cover the bottom. Trim the eggplant and cut crosswise into 18 slices, each about ¼ inch (6 mm) thick. Put the flour, eggs, and bread crumbs into 3 separate shallow bowls or pie pans, and line them up, in that order. Season each bowl with 1 teaspoon salt and a few grinds of pepper. Stir ¼ cup (1 oz/30 g) of the Parmesan into the bread crumbs.

One at a time, dip the eggplant slices in the flour and tap off the excess, and then dip into the eggs and allow the excess to drip off. Finally, dip into the bread crumbs, coating both sides, and place on the prepared pan.

Bake for 15 minutes. Flip the slices over and continue to bake until golden on both sides and tender, about 15 minutes longer. Remove from the oven and let cool for 5–10 minutes. Leave the oven on.

Lightly oil a 9-by-13-inch (23-by-33-cm) baking dish. Overlap the eggplant slices in the prepared dish, placing a piece of mozzarella between the slices. Spoon the sauce evenly over the top and sprinkle with the remaining Parmesan. Bake until the cheese is melted and the sauce is bubbling, about 30 minutes. Let rest for 10 minutes before serving.

¼ cup (2 fl oz/60 ml) extra-virgin olive oil

1 large globe eggplant, about 1½ lb (750 g)

1 cup (5 oz/155 g) all-purpose (plain) flour

3 large eggs, lightly beaten

1¾ cups (7 oz/220 g) plain dried bread crumbs

kosher salt and freshly ground pepper

½ cup (2 oz/60 g) grated Parmesan cheese

½ lb (250 g) fresh mozzarella cheese, cut into 18 pieces

Tomato-Basil Sauce (page 235)

serves 4–6

Freshwater and saltwater. Big and small. Delicate and meaty. And in virtually every color under the sun. Whether fish or shellfish, there is plenty to reap from the sea.

seafood

Fish and shellfish make up an amazing food group that is high in protein, low in fat, and rich in good-for-you omega-3 fatty acids. The twin dangers of overfishing and contaminated waters have placed some limits on both how much and what types of fish and shellfish we should eat. But that's no reason to avoid foods from the sea, lake, or river. There are still many good choices, both farmed and wild, available for all ages and tastes. At our house, we sit down to fish or shellfish—cracked crab, fish tacos, homemade fish sticks, grilled meaty fish steaks—at the dinner table at least once a week, and every one of us looks forward to the meal.

There's a whole hidden world of fish and shellfish out there. Beneath the surface of rivers, lakes, and oceans you'll find more types of sea life than you can possibly imagine. The key to the best is freshness, and a few great recipes.

"one fish, two fish . . ."

Dr. Seuss had it right. Fish come in all shapes, sizes, textures, flavors, and colors, including red and blue. There are wild fish and farmed fish, fish that live in saltwater and fish that live in freshwater. Some have delicate, flaky flesh, and some have rich, meaty flesh. Their flavor depends on what they eat and the amount of fat they carry. Because wild fish feed on an eclectic mix of foods, they taste different all the time. Their farmed cousins were introduced for two reasons: to relieve pressure on wild stocks and to supply the market with fish that are consistent in flavor, size, and texture. In other words, no other protein-rich food is as varied as fish. And all that variety means the door to creativity is wide open when you put it on the menu.

the kindest cuts

Fish come in all sizes but only two body shapes, flat and round. Most small flat fish, like sole and flounder, have delicate, finely flaked flesh and are offered filleted or whole. Halibut, the largest member of the flat fish family, comes in all sizes, from an average of about 25 pounds (12.5 kg) to over 600 pounds (300 kg). It is low in fat, meaty, and is typically sold as fillets, though some smaller specimens are cut into succulent steaks.

Fish markets sell most small round fish, such as cod, mackerel, herring, and farmed catfish and tilapia, as fillets, with farmed striped bass and trout sometimes offered whole. They sell medium round fish, like salmon, as fillets or steaks, and other medium round fish, like yellowtail, mahi mahi, and sturgeon, as fillets. Swordfish, tuna, and other large round fish have huge, thick fillets that are often cut crosswise into boneless meaty steaks.

Firm fillets and small whole fish are great for baking, roasting, broiling, sautéing, and grilling. Delicate flaky fillets are suitable for sautéing and broiling. Meaty steaks can be broiled, sautéed, or grilled. Their firmness makes them easy to handle and less likely to fall apart.

shellfish

Many people who are lukewarm about fish will dive for fresh shellfish, and why not? The sweet meat of shrimp, lobster, and crab is a delectable treat.

shrimp

Shrimp and prawns are technically different—their body structures differ, and they don't even belong to the same species—but nowadays the names are used mainly to denote size, with prawns usually fewer than 15 to a pound (500 g). Anything smaller, 16 to a pound or more, is considered a shrimp. Shrimp are sold by size or count, with large shrimp 16/20 per pound, medium 21/25 and 26/30, and so on. Bay shrimp are a tiny species that live in warm waters along the West Coast.

When shopping, look for wild American shrimp and farmed U.S. shrimp. Shrimp and prawns are sold frozen or thawed, shell on or shell off. Even though they are messy to peel and eat, shrimp cooked in the shell retain more moisture and flavor.

crab

There are East Coast crabs and West Coast crabs, and they are both seasonal. Blue crabs are found along the Atlantic coast, from Nova Scotia down to the Gulf of Mexico, and then on to Argentina. Dungeness crabs live along the Pacific Coast from the Aleutian Islands to California. Florida stone crabs are another tasty

HOW TO MAKE A SHELLFISH BOIL

Select a stainless-steel or other nonreactive pot large enough to hold the shellfish you will be cooking, fill it with water, and bring the water to a rolling boil over high heat. Add 1 sliced yellow onion, the juice of 1 lemon, 2 bay leaves, and 3 tablespoons kosher salt for every 6 qt (6 l) of water. Boil until the onion is tender, about 15 minutes, and then add the shellfish and cook as directed: shrimp and prawns for 4 minutes, or until they are pink and curled; and crab or lobster for 7 minutes for the first pound (500 g) and 3 minutes for each additional pound. Drain well right away, and serve warm or chilled.

choice. They are pulled from the sea, their large claw is removed, and then the crabs are thrown back into the water. The claw grows back and can be harvested again, making the stone crab the poster child for sustainable shellfish.

Crab is sold live, cooked, and as picked meat. It is lots of fun to buy live crabs and cook them yourself. If you are short on time, cooked crabs and picked meat are a convenient option. Be sure to smell them before you buy them to make sure they are impeccably fresh.

lobster

Anyone who likes Maine lobster knows the best time to eat these hearty crustaceans is in the cold winter months, when their meat is sweetest and fills their shells. Most of the meat is in the tail and claws, but if you are diligent, you can get some tasty bites from the smaller legs, too. Spiny lobsters, at home in warmer waters, lack claws, so only their tails are mined for meat. Always buy live lobsters to ensure their freshness. Once they die, their meat deteriorates rapidly.

sustainability

Many watch groups publish lists on sustainability and contamination issues for specific fish species. According to the Monterey Bay Aquarium Seafood Watch, the best and safest wild fish for consumption include Pacific cod and halibut, Alaskan salmon and pollack, Atlantic herring and sardines, and

albacore and skipjack tuna. The best U.S.-farmed fish include arctic char, barramundi, catfish, striped bass, sturgeon, trout, and tilapia.

Other fish are considered good second choices, but limited consumption is advised because of contamination concerns or because of issues as to how they are harvested. These include blue, king, and snow crabs; Pacific sole and flounder; mahi mahi, big eye and yellowfin tuna; and swordfish. Keep in mind that both lists reflect current conditions and are constantly changing, so check a reliable source regularly.

seasonality

Because farming has made fish and shellfish abundant in markets year-round, most shoppers don't think about seasonality when they are at the store. But aficionados eagerly await one fish each year: wild salmon from Alaska and the west coast of the United States. Spring heralds its arrival, and it is a treat to feast on its brightly colored, succulent flesh until we must bid it farewell in the fall. The consistent presence of farmed salmon has confused many of us about when wild fish are available. Buy a piece of each of them and put them to a taste test. The farmed fish is no match for the rich texture and flavor of its wild kin. When wild salmon is out of season, look for it frozen.

Over the years, halibut has been threatened by overfishing, which had reduced its availability to a series of short seasons. But careful fishery management and fishing by quotas have allowed the halibut to bounce back, and it is now available almost year-round.

choosing the freshest

The freshest fish you will ever eat is fish you catch yourself. Like most other foods, the best-tasting fish and shellfish are caught locally. The farther they have to travel, the less fresh they are on arrival. When you live in a landlocked area, the shortest distance from the nearest port or fishery would be your local catch. Also, the word *fresh* means only that the fish was never frozen. It doesn't guarantee quality. I would rather eat fish that was processed and frozen on the boat than fish that was never frozen but is of poor quality.

Fresh fish should never smell fishy. Don't be afraid to ask to sniff fish and shellfish. It's the best way to tell if it is fresh. Look for steaks and fillets that are moist, with no drying or browning around the edges. Whole fish should have bright eyes, pink or red gills, and shiny scales that cling to the skin. Shrimp should feel firm and smell fresh. Make sure that live lobsters and crabs show some movement and lobsters curl their tails tightly when handled.

Buy your fish and shellfish at the end of your shopping trip, so you can get them home right away. If you have some distance to travel and it is a warm day, ask the fishmonger to pack your purchase in ice for the journey. Immediately store the packages in the coldest part of the refrigerator in their original wrapper, and then eat your purchases within two days.

FRESH FISH

Look for these fresh fish at your local fish market or supermarket. At the time of publication, the following fresh fish were recommended. They are either wild caught or sustainably raised. Those listed as U.S. were caught in U.S. waters under EPA guidelines.

WILD	FARMED
Pacific flounder	Arctic char
Pacific sole	Sturgeon
Halibut	Striped bass
Salmon (May to October)	Tilapia
Tuna (albacore and skipjack)	Catfish
Pacific cod	Trout
U.S. Mahi mahi	Yellowtail
U.S. Pacific swordfish	
Herring	
Sardines	

smoked salmon

Once you smoke a salmon fillet, you will never again spend your hard-earned dollars on the pricey store-bought stuff. Salmon's high fat content makes it a great candidate, but lean fish like halibut, sturgeon, and delicate trout can be hot smoked, too. And the fish can be fresh or frozen. Freezing draws out moisture, which gives the smoked fish a firmer texture.

My favorite wood for smoked salmon is alder, which has a sweet, subtle flavor. Almond and cherry are also good. Use finely chipped wood, not sawdust, and make sure you use natural, untreated wood chips without additives.

This salmon is a great topper for bagels and makes a delicious appetizer served with crème fraîche and seeded-rye toasts. For a little spice, press some coarsely ground pepper into the flesh of the salmon when it's fresh out of the brine, before it goes in the refrigerator.

make a homemade stove-top smoker

You can quickly and easily make your very own homemade stove-top smoker by following these steps.

what you'll need

- a large, heavy frying pan
- a second shallow, sturdy metal pan, such as a pie or cake pan, that fits inside the frying pan
- aluminum foil
- fine wood chips
- a round wire rack that fits over the smaller, second pan

how to make it

Line both pans with the foil. Place a handful of fine wood chips in the center of the larger pan.

Place the smaller pan directly on top of the pile of wood chips to flatten them.

Follow project steps 1–3 (page 160). When the fish is ready to smoke, place the oiled rack with the fish on it over the smaller pan, and seal the frying pan tightly with foil.

Place the smoker on the burner and proceed as directed in step 4 (page 161).

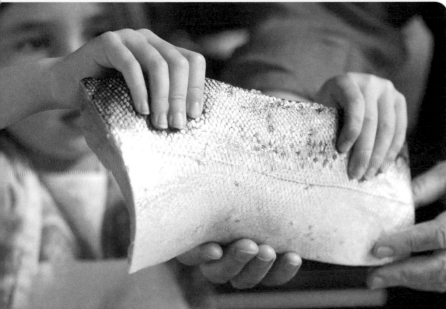

what you'll need to make smoked salmon

- 5 cups (40 fl oz/1.25 l) cold water

- a glass baking dish large enough to hold the fish and brine

- 1 cup (5oz/155 g) kosher salt

- ¾ cup (6 oz/185 g) firmly packed golden brown sugar

- a whisk

- 1 wild salmon fillet, 1½ lb (750 g) and about 1 inch thick, with skin intact

- 2–3 small plates for weighting fish down

- vegetable oil for rack

- fine natural alder wood chips or chips of choice

1 make the brine

Pour the water into the glass baking dish. Add the salt and sugar to the water and stir with the whisk until dissolved.

2 brine the fish

Place the fish, skin side up, in the brine. Weight the fish with the plates to submerge it in the brine. Refrigerate for 2 hours.

3 dry the fish

Rinse the fish with cold water and gently pat it dry with paper towels. Lightly oil the smoker rack and place the fish on it. Place the fish, unwrapped, in the refrigerator until it dries and forms a shiny skin, at least 2 hours or up to overnight.

4 get the smoker ready

Ready a store-bought smoker according to the manufacturer's instructions or a homemade smoker (page 159). Place the fish in the smoker and cover, then place the smoker on the stove top.

5 smoke the fish

Turn your exhaust fan on to high speed. Turn on the burner to medium heat and cook for 20–25 minutes. The fish will start to ooze white juice when it is done. Press the edge of the fillet lightly with your fingertip; if it flakes easily it is done. Be careful not to overcook.

6 eat it up!

Uncover the fish, lift the rack out with 2 pairs of tongs, and let the fish cool slightly. Put the rack with the fish, uncovered, in the refrigerator until chilled. (This is easier than trying to remove hot fish from a hot rack.) Remove the chilled fish from the rack and wrap tightly in plastic wrap. Use within 3 days or freeze for up to 3 months.

Miniature or full sized, these sandwiches are layered with flavor, pure fun to make, and perfect for a bagel brunch party. Just line up the herbed cream cheese, a selection of toasted bagels, the sliced vegetables, and the salmon and give each kid a spreader and let them go to town. The adults get so excited about these delicious morning treats that they are almost like kids themselves.

bagel sandwiches

½ lb (250 g) whipped cream cheese

1 tablespoon chopped fresh dill

2 tablespoons chopped fresh chives

2 tablespoons drained capers, chopped

1 tablespoon fresh lemon juice

kosher salt and freshly ground pepper

4–6 onion, poppy seed, or whole wheat (wholemeal) bagels

½ English (hothouse) cucumber, sliced very thin

½–¾ lb (250–375 g) hot-smoked salmon, flaked

thinly sliced red onion (optional)

makes 4–6 sandwiches

In a bowl, combine the cream cheese, dill, chives, capers, and lemon juice and mix well. Season to taste with salt and pepper. The mix might not need any salt because of the saltiness of the ingredients.

Split and toast the bagels. Spread the cut sides of the bagels with the cream cheese mixture, using about 1½ tablespoons on each.

Arrange the cucumber slices in a flower pattern on top of the cream cheese on the bottom half of each bagel, placing 1 cucumber slice over the hole.

Divide the salmon evenly among the cucumber-topped bagel halves, and then top with the onions, if using. Close the bagels and press down gently to secure the filling. Serve right away.

My husband and I like our shrimp spicy, and our daughters don't, so I split the bread crumbs between two pans and add some cayenne to our half. The kids get shrimp seasoned with salt only. Everyone is happy. These crispy shrimp are a snap to make. Double or triple the recipe as an appetizer for a crowd.

crispy shrimp with real lemony mayo

To make the mayo, in a heatproof bowl, whisk together the egg yolk and lemon juice. Set the bowl over (not touching) boiling water in a saucepan and whisk until the yolk is fluffy and hot, about 20 seconds. Do not allow to scramble. Remove from the heat and continue to whisk to cool down. Whisk in the mustard, salt, and sugar. Combine the canola oil and 2 tablespoons olive oil in a liquid measuring cup. Place the bowl with the egg mixture on a damp towel to keep it from moving around. Slowly drizzle the oils into the yolk mixture while whisking vigorously. Continue to whisk until shiny and thick. Taste and adjust the seasoning, then cover and refrigerate for up to 2 days. You should have about ½ cup (4 fl oz/125 ml).

Preheat the oven to 425°F (220°C). Pour the ¼ cup of oil into a rimmed baking sheet. Put the flour, egg whites, and bread crumbs into 3 separate shallow bowls and line them up, in that order. Season each with 1 teaspoon salt.

One at a time, dip the shrimp into the flour and tap off the excess, and then dip into the egg whites and allow the excess to drip off. Finally, roll in the bread crumbs and place on the prepared pan, spacing them apart. (At this point, the shrimp can be refrigerated, uncovered, for a few hours. The coating will dry out a bit, and crisp better.) Bake for 5 minutes. Turn the shrimp over and continue to bake until golden and curled, 5–6 minutes longer. Transfer to a platter and serve right away with the mayo for dipping.

for the lemony mayo

1 large egg yolk

1 tablespoon lemon juice

½ teaspoon Dijon mustard

¼ teaspoon kosher salt

¼ teaspoon sugar

½ cup (4 fl oz/125 ml) canola oil

2 tablespoons olive oil

¼ cup (2 fl oz/60 ml) olive oil

½ cup (2½ oz/75 g) all-purpose (plain) flour

3 large egg whites, lightly beaten

1½ cups (6 oz/185 g) plain fine bread crumbs

kosher salt

12 large shrimp, peeled and deveined, with tails intact

serves 4

My kids enjoy these cakes because there is not a lot of "stuff" mixed in with the crabmeat. When combining the ingredients, handle the mixture gently, or you will be left with threads of crabmeat and no chunks. Cook them gently, too, to avoid overbrowning. The center only needs to be warm, not burning hot.

citrus crabby cakes

½ lb (250 g) fresh-cooked crabmeat, picked over for shell fragments and cartilage

I cup (2 oz/60 g) fresh white bread crumbs

¼ cup (2 fl oz/60 ml) store-bought mayonnaise or Lemony Mayo (page 165)

I tablespoon chopped fresh chives

kosher salt and freshly ground pepper

I tablespoon unsalted butter

watercress or butter lettuce leaves, for serving

I Meyer lemon, cut into wedges, for serving

citrus vinaigrette, homemade (page 280) or store-bought (optional)

serves 4–6

In a bowl, combine the crabmeat, bread crumbs, mayonnaise, and chives, and mix gently until the ingredients are evenly distributed, being careful not to break up the chunks of crabmeat. Season to taste with salt and pepper. Shape into 6 equal-sized cakes and place them on a plate. Cover and refrigerate for at least 10 minutes or up to overnight to allow the breadcrumbs to absorb some of the juices.

Heat a sauté pan over medium-high heat and add the butter. When the butter is hot, add the crab cakes and cook until golden on the undersides, 3–4 minutes. Flip the cakes over and cook on the second sides until golden, 3–4 minutes longer, reducing the heat if needed to avoiding overcooking the exterior.

Transfer to a platter, garnish with the watercress and lemon wedges, and drizzle the vinaigrette over the top, if using. Serve right away.

With the exception of a drizzle of sour cream, these tacos are almost fat free. But because they are so light and delicious, it is hard to limit yourself to just one or two. I set up the components as a buffet. Just line up small bowls full of lime wedges, sour cream, fresh cilantro (fresh coriander) leaves, and salsa or hot pepper sauce along with the slaw. That way, everyone can decide what they want on their tacos.

fish tacos with slaw

To make the slaw, in a large bowl, combine both cabbages, cilantro, green onion, lime juice, sugar, ½ teaspoon salt, and cayenne and mix well. Let stand at room temperature for 20 minutes, then taste and adjust the seasoning. For the best flavor, cover and refrigerate for about 1 hour before serving.

Prepare a medium-hot fire in a charcoal or gas grill. Make sure the grill rack is clean, then oil it and let the oil burn off for 5 minutes.

Lightly brush the fish on both sides with the oil and then season on both sides with salt and pepper. Place on the grill rack and cook, turning once, until browned on both sides and opaque throughout, 3–4 minutes on each side. Transfer to a plate and divide into 12 equal pieces, discarding any errant bones.

Wrap the tortillas in aluminum foil and place on top of the grill to warm while the fish is cooking, turning occasionally.

To assemble each taco, place a warm tortilla on a plate, top with a piece of fish, a squeeze of lime, a little slaw, a drizzle of sour cream, a cilantro sprig, and a few drops of hot sauce (see note above).

for the slaw

1 cup (3 oz/90 g) finely shredded red cabbage

4 cups (12 oz/375 g) finely shredded green cabbage

3 tablespoons chopped fresh cilantro (fresh coriander)

¼ cup (¾ oz/20 g) chopped green (spring) onion

2 tablespoons lime juice

½ teaspoon sugar

kosher salt

⅛ teaspoon cayenne

canola oil

1 lb (500 g) firm white fish fillets such as cod, snapper, or mahi mahi

freshly ground pepper

12 corn tortillas, homemade (page 35) or store-bought

serves 4–6

Garlic has the chutzpah to stand up to grilled, meaty fish steaks, but I ease up on it a little when I'm cooking for kids because sometimes their little taste buds can be easily overwhelmed by its intensity. To satisfy adults, I serve the fish with a deliciously spicy garlic sauce.

grilled garlicky fish

1 clove garlic, pressed

2 tablespoons olive oil

1 teaspoon chopped fresh thyme

1 teaspoon lemon zest

kosher salt and freshly ground pepper

1½ lb (750 g) halibut or other meaty white fish, 1 inch (2.5 cm) thick

for the spicy garlic sauce

3 tablespoons olive oil

2 tablespoons lemon juice

1 clove garlic, pressed

3 tablespoons finely chopped fresh flat-leaf (Italian) parsley

½ teaspoon kosher salt

red pepper flakes

vegetable oil for grill rack

lemon wedges for serving

serves 4–6

In a small bowl, stir together the garlic, oil, thyme, lemon zest, and a few grinds of pepper. Place the fish in a shallow glass or ceramic dish and rub it on both sides with the garlic mixture. Cover and refrigerate for at least 1 hour or up to overnight.

Meanwhile, make the garlic sauce. In a small bowl, whisk together the oil, lemon juice, garlic, parsley, salt, and pepper flakes to taste. Set aside until serving, then taste and adjust the seasoning.

Prepare a medium-hot fire in a charcoal or gas grill. Make sure the grill rack is clean, then oil it and let the oil burn off for 5 minutes. Season the fish on both sides with salt. Place on the grill rack and cook, turning once, until browned on both sides and almost cooked through, 4–5 minutes on each side. Transfer to a platter and let rest for 5 minutes (the fish will finish cooking off the grill). Serve with the lemon wedges and the sauce.

My kids have always liked anything seasoned with lemon and salt, so this recipe—with its one-two punch of lemon and capers—is a favorite of theirs. I like it because I can prep all of the ingredients ahead of time and then, at dinnertime, I can cook and serve the dish in about 10 minutes.

panfried sole with lemon-caper sauce

Put the flour in a shallow bowl or pie pan. Season a piece of fish on both sides with salt and pepper, and then coat on both sides with the flour, tapping off the excess. Set aside on a plate and repeat with the remaining fish.

Heat a large sauté pan over medium-high heat and add 2 tablespoons of the butter. When the butter begins to brown, add the fish and cook, turning once, until golden brown on both sides and opaque throughout, 2–3 minutes on each side. If the flour begins to burn, reduce the heat slightly. Transfer to a platter and keep warm.

Add 1 tablespoon of the butter to the pan over medium-high heat. When it begins to brown, add the shallot and capers and sauté until the shallot is lightly browned, 1–2 minutes. Add the wine and the lemon zest and juice and bring to a boil, stirring to dislodge any browned bits from the bottom. Boil until reduced by half, about 2 minutes. Remove from the heat and whisk in the remaining 5 tablespoons (2½ oz/75 g) butter. Season to taste with salt and pepper. Spoon the sauce over the fish and serve right away.

½ cup (2½ oz/75 g) all-purpose (plain) flour

6 sole or tilapia fillets

kosher salt and freshly ground white pepper

½ cup (4 oz/125 g) unsalted butter

1 tablespoon minced shallot

1 heaping tablespoon drained capers

¼ cup (2 fl oz/60 ml) dry white wine

½ teaspoon grated lemon zest

2 tablespoons fresh lemon juice

serves 4–6

It doesn't matter whether you cut the fish into serving portions or into sticks. The kids think the fish sticks are cool and the adults think they taste good, no matter what the shape. I add a bit of cayenne to the cornmeal because my kids don't mind the touch of spice and the cornmeal seems to offset the heat but not the flavor.

crispy cornmeal fish with tartar sauce

½ cup (4 fl oz/125 ml) store-bought mayonnaise or Lemony Mayo (page 165)

¼ cup (1½ oz/45 g) finely chopped bread and butter pickles, homemade (page 137) or store-bought

2 tablespoons finely chopped fresh flat-leaf (Italian) parsley

2 teaspoons drained capers, chopped

½ teaspoon cayenne

kosher salt

1½ lb (750 g) thick tilapia, cod, or catfish fillets

1 cup (5 oz/155 g) all-purpose (plain) flour

3 large egg whites, beaten

1 cup fine-grind cornmeal

extra-virgin olive oil

lemon wedges for serving

serves 4–6

To make the tartar sauce, in a small bowl, stir together the mayonnaise, pickles, 1 tablespoon parsley, capers, and ¼ teaspoon cayenne. Season to taste with salt, then taste and add more cayenne if you want it spicier.

You can cut the fish into 4–6 uniform pieces, or you can cut the fish into strips 1 inch (2.5 cm) wide, to make fish sticks. The cooking method is the same for both. Put ½ cup (2.5 oz/75 g) flour, the egg whites, and the cornmeal plus the remaining ½ cup flour into 3 separate shallow bowls, and line them up, in that order. Season each bowl with 1 teaspoon salt. Stir the remaining cayenne and the remaining parsley into the cornmeal bowl.

One at a time, coat the fish pieces on both sides with the flour and tap off the excess, and then dip into the egg whites and allow the excess to drip off. Finally, dip into the cornmeal mixture, coating both sides, and place on a plate.

Heat a large sauté pan over medium-high heat and add 2–3 tablespoons oil. When the oil is hot, add as many fish pieces as will fit without crowding and cook, turning once, until golden on both sides and opaque throughout, 3–4 minutes on each side. Transfer to a warmed platter and keep warm while you cook the remaining fish. Serve the fish right away with the tartar sauce and lemon wedges.

A fragrant, golden brown roasted chicken with crisp skin and juicy meat on the Sunday dinner table is guaranteed to make kids and adults alike clamor for their favorite pieces.

chicken

Chickens were pecking and scratching around in the fresh air of India and East Asia as far back as 7,000 BC. And whoever decided to snare that first bird, pluck its feathers, and roast it started a trend that has never slowed. Nowadays, poultry is eaten around the world, and the chicken is the belle of the ball. But that's no surprise. Chickens taste good, are low in fat, are relatively inexpensive, and can be seasoned with dozens of different herbs and spices. You can cook them whole or in parts, on or off the bone, in the oven, on the stove top, or on the grill. You can eat chicken hot or cold, and the meat is great in a sandwich, tucked into a potpie, or tossed in a salad. Even the bones come in handy for making a big pot of stock.

While chicken is an easy, always-pleasing weeknight standby, it doesn't mean that it has to be boring. Stuff pitas and pies with it, or simmer it in curries or soups. Out of time? Roast it whole with a sprinkle of salt and herbs.

the number-one meat

Chicken is the number-one meat consumed in the United States, beating pork, beef, and lamb by a mile. Most of the chickens sold are products of strict breeding programs designed to ensure a high meat to bone ratio, as few feathers as possible, and fast growth (see the sidebar to the right). They are typically a cross between White Rock, a New England breed, and Cornish, a traditional British breed. But there is growing interest in two areas: heritage breeds, which were popular in the past but fell out of favor when they didn't easily transfer to factory farms, and natural, free range, and organic birds.

what's in a name?

You might think that all chickens are alike, but you would be wrong. Chickens can vary wildly in flavor depending on how they are raised. Simply put, there are much better choices than the bland, fatty supermarket birds that are fed a diet of antibiotic-laced grain in a crowded pen on a factory farm.

Three terms are used to indicate a higher-quality chicken: natural, free range, and organic. Natural means that no additives were added in processing. It does not mean the birds were raised without antibiotics. Free-range chickens are raised in pens with access to the outdoors, but how far they can or do roam is not specified. They are leaner than factory-raised chickens and have more flavor, so even though they cost more, you are paying for meat, not extra fat. They are also sometimes labeled antibiotic free, though the claim does not have to be verified by anyone other than the farmer.

Like free-range chickens, organic birds must have access to the outdoors. But they must also be raised on an antibiotic-free diet of organic grains and whatever bugs they can scratch for. If you are concerned about pesticide or other residues in feed, then this is the chicken for you.

turkey

Turkey is the bird of both celebration and sandwiches. It comes whole, sliced into boneless cutlets, halved, quartered, in parts, and ground. The Broad-breasted White turkey, with a meaty breast so large that it dwarfs the rest of the bird, is the breed most widely available to consumers. Narragansett and Red Bourbon are two examples of heritage breeds that have smaller breasts and tastier meat. The same labels—natural, free range, and organic—that apply to chickens apply to turkeys.

There is no gender discrimination when it comes to deciding on which turkey to consume. Both toms and hens are sold for meat. Hens usually weigh under 16 pounds (8 kg) and toms usually weigh about 16 pounds or more. Many cooks prefer the smaller hen because it is easier to handle. Toms have bigger bones and more inedible portions. Tenderness, however, is determined by age, not gender. The older they get, the tougher they are.

other poultry

It seems that the less popular you are, the less people actually want to mess with you. Instead, they enjoy you for what you are, rather than who you might become. For that reason, birds such as ducks, geese, guinea hens, and squabs have not been overbred, which means they are closer to their wild cousins than chickens and turkeys are to theirs.

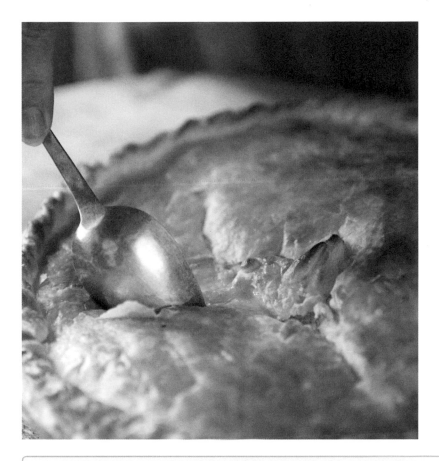

WHERE ARE ITS FEATHERS?

Several years ago, our family visited an Oregon farmer who had a good business selling organic pasture-raised chickens to the local community. As we walked toward a movable electric fence, the farmer explained that the birds were sensitive to cold, and that when they were moved, they had to be facing the direction that provided the most warmth from the sun. I soon realized why. The chickens were small, quite pink, and almost featherless. The reason? Fewer feathers made them easier to process. I was shocked. But then I realized that my image of a heavily feathered, brightly colored eating chicken was actually a laying chicken. All chickens raised for meat are white feathered. Dark feathers grow from dark skin, and no one wants to buy any chicken that doesn't have perfect pink or yellow skin.

In general, these birds are more often found in restaurant kitchens than home kitchens, especially guinea hens and squabs. Some folks are put off by talk of the fat content of ducks and geese. But they are delicious when cooked properly. For the best results, cook the breasts and legs separately, roasting the breasts and braising the legs for optimum enjoyment. Guinea hens can be cooked like a chicken. Their skin crisps up beautifully. Squabs have rich, flavor-packed red meat. Roast them to medium, not well done, for the best texture.

keep it moist

Poultry, with the exception of duck and goose, tends to be lean with little extra fat to protect the meat, especially breast meat, from drying out. The use of a few techniques before cooking and choosing the right cooking method will make dry, rubbery chicken and turkey a thing of the past.

Breading, marinating, and brining helps poultry stay moist and flavorful. Breading as simple as egg and flour forms a crunchy coat that seals in the juices. This technique works especially well on boneless, skinless chicken breasts that are quick cooking and low fat. All parts of the chicken benefit from marinating. Try a simple marinade of good-quality olive oil infused with herbs and aromatics such as garlic and onions. Marinating in buttermilk or yogurt tenderizes poultry with its dairy acid and also can serve to marry the flavor of herbs and spices with the meat. The moist yogurt-marinated Chicken Kebabs (page 194) are a wonderful example of this technique. Brining poultry in a mixture of water and salt plumps the meat cells and gives them extra insurance against drying out. Brine also has the added benefit of seasoning the meat throughout, and if you add spices, aromatics, herbs or sugar those flavors will also be imparted into the meat. Brine whole birds overnight and chicken parts for up to 6 hours for optimum benefit. For a basic brine, mix 1 gallon of cold water with ½ cup kosher salt. Stir until the salt dissolves. Try brining your next herb-roasted chicken. Stuff the herbs under the breast after you remove the bird from the brine and pat it dry, then roast.

Pounding or slicing tender breast meat into thin pieces allows it to stay tender and moist when simmered in a fragrant broth, such as in the Chicken-coconut Curry (page 191), or when cooked over high heat in a sauté pan. The Turkey Saltimbocca (page 193) would not be nearly as delicious if it wasn't for this quick method. Cooking lean cuts using moist methods, such as baking in parchment paper or poaching, will yield juicy meat almost every time. Choose your cut, its preparation and cooking method wisely and your poultry will always be moist and flavorful.

buying and storing poultry

It's nice to know that all of the parts come from the same chicken. To ensure this, buy whole birds and ask the butcher to cut them up. Boneless, skinless breasts are convenient, but they have the least amount of flavor. If possible, choose organic, locally raised birds for the best flavor. Buy poultry that looks fresh and moist and is free of off odors. Packaging should be tightly wrapped and show no signs of damage. Poultry is often packed in ice for shipping, so packaged meat sometimes appears frozen. It is the water in the poultry that is frozen, not the meat, so technically it is still a fresh product and this chilling should not affect its quality. Purchase poultry at the end of your shopping trip, and then place it in the coldest part of the refrigerator the moment you get home. Keep it in the store packaging to limit bacterial contamination from repeated handling.

Cook raw poultry within two days of purchase, and refrigerate cooked poultry no longer than four days. Wash your hands and all work surfaces and tools with hot, soapy water after preparing any bird, and allow boards and knives to air dry to avoid contaminating dish towels.

CHICKENS, BY SIZE AND AGE

- **Poussin:** Immature bird 4 to 5 weeks old and weighing less than 2 pounds (1 kg).

- **Rock Cornish game hen:** Immature bird 5 to 6 weeks old and weighing 1 to 2 pounds (500 g to 1 kg). Usually roasted whole (sometimes stuffed) or butterflied and grilled.

- **Broiler-fryer:** Tender bird about 7 weeks old and weighing 3 to 5 pounds (1.5 to 2.5 kg). Most packaged chicken parts are from this size. Good cooked by any method.

- **Roaster:** Usually 3 to 5 months old and weighing 6 to 8 pounds (3 to 4 kg). Usually roasted whole.

- **Capon:** Castrated rooster 4 to 8 months old and weighing 5 to 7 pounds (2.5 to 3.5 kg), with large, meaty breasts and tender meat. Usually roasted whole.

- **Stewing chicken:** Mature hen more than 10 months old and weighing 5 to 6 pounds (2.5 to 3 kg). Good for braising and stocks.

- **Cock or rooster:** Tough, old male bird of varying weight. Good for making authentic *coq au vin,* but not much else except stock.

chicken stock

Chicken stock is the foundation for so many good things to eat that you want to make the best stock possible. And although making stock is easy, it has become a lost art. Convenient-to-use boxes of broth have pushed it aside along with your memories of homemade chicken soup. Make homemade stock a family affair by enlisting the children to peel the vegetables and pick the warm meat from the bones while you tend the stockpot.

This stock is actually more of a cross between a stock and a broth. Stock is usually made with bones and a little meat, while broth is made with more meat and fewer bones. Stock is rich with the gelatin and flavor extracted from the bones, while broth is more delicate and doesn't thicken when reduced. Using a whole chicken gives this stock a delicate flavor and yields perfectly cooked moist meat for chicken soup, potpies, or chicken salad.

roasted chicken stock

Roasted chicken stock is rich and dark. Use this as an all-purpose stock for making sauces and for braising all types of meat.

Because you roast the chicken and use primarily bony parts, the stock has a deep flavor and color, making it a good stand-in for beef, veal, or duck stock. For lamb, add roasted lamb scraps to the stock to lend their distinctive flavor.

how to make it

Substitute 5 lb (2.5 kg) chicken bones, such as wings, backs, and necks, for the whole chicken in the Chicken Stock project (page 182).

Preheat the oven to 400°F (200°C).

Spread the chicken bones in a large roasting pan and roast in the oven until golden brown, 30–40 minutes.

Transfer the roasted chicken bones to a large stockpot.

Drain off the fat from the roasting pan, and put the pan on the stove top over high heat. Add 2 cups (16 fl oz/ 500 ml) red or white wine and bring to a boil. Use a spatula to scrape up the flavorful browned bits stuck to the pan bottom.

Pour the wine over the bones in the stockpot and add the vegetables and water as directed in step 1 (page 182).

Bring to a boil, skim, reduce the heat, and simmer for 4 hours. Then strain and chill for a very rich and gelatinous stock.

what you'll need to make chicken stock

- 1 organic chicken, 4–5 lb (2–2.5 g), quartered
- 3 carrots, peeled and cut in half
- 1 celery stalk, trimmed and cut in half
- 1 yellow onion, quartered
- handful of fresh flat-leaf (Italian) parsley sprigs
- 1 large bay leaf
- 1 tablespoon kosher salt
- 8-qt (8-l) stockpot
- large metal ladle or spoon
- 2 storage containers (for meat and stock)
- fine-mesh sieve

1 put it in the pot

Place the chicken, all of the vegetables, and the parsley, bay leaf, and kosher salt in the stockpot and add water to cover by 2 inches (5 cm).

2 simmer it slowly

Bring to a boil over medium-high heat, then reduce the heat to low. Use the ladle or spoon to skim off any foam that forms on the surface. Simmer, uncovered, for 45 minutes, continuing to skim the surface as the fat rises to the top.

3 pick the meat

Remove the breasts from the
stock and continue to simmer
for 30 minutes, then remove the
remaining chicken pieces. Pick
the meat off the bones and return
the bones to the pot, adding water
if needed to keep the ingredients
submerged. Place the meat in a
sealed container and refrigerate.

4 strain the stock

Continue to simmer the stock
for 45 minutes longer, skimming
as needed. Place a sieve over
a large container and strain the
stock through the sieve into
the container. Let cool to room
temperature, then place it in the
refrigerator, uncovered, to chill.

5 store the stock

After the stock is cold, seal the
container tightly with a lid. The
stock will be rich and gelatinous.
It will keep for up to 1 week
in the refrigerator or up to
3 months in the freezer. Lift off
and discard any fat solidified on
the surface before using.

At the sound of the slightest sniffle, a pot of this hearty, delicious chicken soup goes onto the stove. I am convinced it has halted many a cold in our house. And once you have good stock—which you can make in big batches and store easily in the freezer—making this classic soup is a snap.

chicken soup

I tablespoon extra-virgin olive oil

3 medium carrots, sliced

I small yellow onion, finely chopped

I stalk celery, sliced

6 cups (48 fl oz/1.5 l) chicken stock (page 180)

2 cups (12 oz/375 g) shredded or diced cooked chicken

2 cups cooked pasta shapes or rice (optional)

kosher salt and freshly ground pepper

serves 4–6

Heat a large saucepan over medium-high heat and add the oil. When the oil is hot, add the carrots, onion, and celery, and sauté the vegetables until they have softened and released some of their moisture, about 2–3 minutes.

Add the stock and bring to a boil. Reduce the heat to low and simmer gently, uncovered, until the vegetables are tender, about 20 minutes.

Add the chicken and pasta, if using, and simmer until heated through, about 5 minutes. Season to taste with salt and pepper. Ladle into warmed bowls and serve right away.

get creative

For Italian-Style Chicken Soup, follow this recipe, adding a 2-inch (5-cm) Parmesan cheese rind and 1 bay leaf with the stock. Then add 1 tablespoon finely chopped fresh flat-leaf (Italian) parsley and cooked acini di pepe (peppercorns) pasta at the end.

For Chicken Soup, Middle Eastern Style, follow this recipe, using rice instead of pasta and adding 2 tablespoons chopped fresh dill and 3 tablespoons lemon juice at the end.

For The Cure, Italian Style, my mother's medicine for a stomachache, simmer a 2-inch (5-cm) Parmesan cheese rind in plain chicken stock for 30 minutes. Then add cooked stelline (little stars) pasta at the end. Serve with grated Parmesan.

There are four keys to a golden, crisp-skinned, juicy and flavorful chicken: 1) Start with a high-quality bird (page 176). 2) Season it correctly. 3) Cook it at a high temperature for the ideal amount of time for its weight. 4) Let it rest before you carve it. Save any leftovers for making the potpie on page 188.

herb-roasted chicken

Preheat the oven to 425°F (220°C). Cut off the chicken's tail with kitchen scissors. Remove the giblets and reserve for another use or discard, and remove the excess skin and fat from the cavity and neck.

In a small bowl, stir together the chopped rosemary, thyme, sage, and ¼ cup (2 fl oz/60 ml) oil and season with pepper. With the shoulders facing you, gently separate the skin from the meat with your fingers, being careful not to tear the skin. Rotate the bird 180 degrees, and loosen the skin above the cavity the same way, reaching in as far as possible to loosen the skin on the tops of the thighs and legs. Slip the herb mixture between the skin and flesh, and rub it evenly over the exposed meat, covering it as much as possible. Pat the skin back into place, and tuck the wing tips under the shoulders.

Season the cavity with 2 teaspoons salt, and then stuff with the herb sprigs, onion, and garlic, pushing them in as far as they will go. Tie the legs together with kitchen string. (The chicken can be prepared up to this point a day in advance, wrapped well, and refrigerated.) Rub the entire bird with oil and season well with salt. Put breast side up in a roasting pan.

Roast the chicken until the juices run clear when the thigh is pierced, about 1 hour and 10 minutes (12–15 minutes per lb/500 g), or a thermometer inserted in the thickest part of the thigh not touching bone registers 165°F (75°C). Let rest 15 minutes before carving.

1 roasting chicken,
4–5 lb (2–2.5 kg)

2 teaspoons chopped
fresh rosemary, plus
1 sprig, 4 inches
(10 cm) long

1 tablespoon chopped
fresh thyme, plus
3 bushy sprigs

2 teaspoons chopped
fresh sage, plus 1 sprig

extra-virgin olive oil

kosher salt and freshly
ground pepper

½ small yellow onion

3 large cloves garlic

serves 4–6

This beautiful golden puffy potpie creates a stir of excitement in my house. My daughters help me cover the pie with puff pastry, then they go to town decorating it with chickens, flowers, and other shapes cut from pastry scraps. They love to admire their handiwork once the pie is baked. In a hurry? Just cut the pastry round to fit inside the baking dish edge and lay it over the filling without sealing, then let it bake as usual.

golden chicken potpie

1 tablespoon unsalted butter

½ yellow onion, diced

1 stalk celery, finely sliced

2 small carrots, sliced

1 cup mushroom caps, quartered

¼ cup (2 fl oz/60 ml) dry white wine

1 cup (8 fl oz/250 ml) chicken stock (page 180)

½ teaspoon chopped fresh thyme

1 tablespoon plus 1 teaspoon all-purpose (plain) flour

2 cups (12 oz/375 g) diced cooked chicken

⅓ recipe Quick Puff Pastry (page 279), or 1 sheet all-butter frozen puff pastry, 10-by-13 inches (25-by-33 cm), thawed

1 large egg beaten with 1 teaspoon water

serves 4–6

Heat a saucepan over medium-high heat and warm the butter. Add the onion and celery and sauté until golden, 2–3 minutes. Add the carrots and mushrooms and sauté 3 minutes. Pour in the wine, bring it to a simmer, and reduce for 3 minutes. Add the stock and thyme and simmer until the vegetables are crisp-tender, about 5 minutes.

In a small bowl, whisk together the flour and ¼ cup (2 fl oz/60 ml) cold water until smooth. Whisk about ¼ cup of the hot stock from the pan into the flour mixture, and then pour through a fine-mesh sieve back into the pan, stir well, and bring to a boil. Reduce the heat to medium-low and simmer until the vegetables are just tender, about 5 minutes. Add the diced chicken, return to a boil, then reduce the heat and simmer for 5 minutes to heat the chicken through. Remove from the heat and pour into a bowl, let cool, cover, and refrigerate for 2 hours. The filling can be made up to 2 days in advance.

Preheat the oven to 400°F (200°C). Butter a 9-inch (23-cm) pie dish. Pour the filling into the dish. On a floured work surface, roll the pastry into a 12-inch (30-cm) circle. Brush the top and bottom of the edge of the dish with the egg. Lay the dough over the filling and trim so it hangs 1½ inches over the edge. Wrap the dough around the edge and press firmly. Crimp the dough against the lip of the dish with the tines of a fork. Refrigerate for 20 minutes to relax the dough. Brush the top of the pie with the egg. Cut a few vents in the center. Bake until the crust is golden and the filling is hot and bubbling, about 45 minutes. Let cool for 15 minutes before serving.

I have a kaffir lime tree planted up against a stone wall in my garden, which keeps my kitchen in lime leaves for this robust curry. My kids think this curry is exotic, and they love the limey-coconut flavor that falls somewhere between tangy and sweet. If your family likes spicy curry, add thinly sliced serrano chiles. Serve the curry over rice with bowls of lime wedges, bean sprouts, and sprigs of fresh cilantro (fresh coriander).

chicken-coconut curry

Peel and thinly slice the onion. Trim the lemongrass to the white bulb only, then slice in half lengthwise and crush it with the side of your knife. Heat a saucepan over medium-high heat and add the oil. When the oil is hot, add the onion, lemongrass, ginger, and garlic, and sauté until the garlic is golden, 1–2 minutes. Add the cumin, sliced chiles (if using; see note above) and brown sugar, and cook until the sugar bubbles, about 30 seconds. Add the coconut milk, stock, fish sauce, and lime leaves and bring to a boil. Reduce the heat to low, and simmer for 15 minutes to blend the flavors.

Add the chicken, basil, mushrooms, and lime juice, and simmer until the chicken is opaque, about 10 minutes longer. Remove and discard the lemongrass stalks. Serve the curry over steamed jasmine rice and garnish with cilantro sprigs, lime wedges, and bean sprouts (see note above). Serve right away.

1 small yellow onion

2 lemongrass stalks

2 tablespoons canola oil

1 heaping tablespoon grated fresh ginger

2 cloves garlic, pressed

¼ teaspoon ground cumin

1 tablespoon firmly packed light brown sugar

1 can (14.5 fl oz/430 ml) coconut milk

½ cup (4 fl oz/125 ml) chicken stock (page 180)

2–3 tablespoons fish sauce

2 kaffir lime leaves

1 lb (500 g) boneless, skinless chicken breasts or thighs, thinly sliced

½ cup (¾ oz/20 g) firmly packed fresh basil leaves

1 cup (3 oz/90 g) thinly sliced white mushrooms

2 tablespoons lime juice

serves 4–6

My kids help me shred the carrots and chicken for this bursting-with-flavor, vegetable-packed salad. After I ready the remaining ingredients, they toss everything together. I make the Thai vinaigrette on page 280 without the chile, remove a portion for them, then add the chile to the rest.

asian chicken salad

7 oz (220 g) dried, thin-ribbon rice noodles

2½ cups (15 oz/470 g) cooked shredded chicken breast meat

3 cups (9 oz/280 g) shredded napa cabbage

1 cup (3½ oz/105 g) shredded carrot

2 cups (10 oz/315 g) thinly sliced cucumber

¼ cup (1 oz/30 g) thinly sliced green (spring) onion

½ cup (⅓ oz/10 g) chopped fresh cilantro (fresh coriander)

¼ cup (⅓ oz/10 g) *each* torn fresh basil leaves and fresh mint leaves

Thai lime vinaigrette, homemade (page 280) or store-bought

salted dry-roasted peanuts

lime wedges for serving

serves 4–6

Bring a saucepan three-fourths full of water to a boil, add the noodles, and remove from the heat. Let soak until tender, 8–10 minutes. Drain into a large sieve, rinse under cold running water, and then drain well again.

In a large bowl, combine the noodles, chicken, cabbage, carrot, cucumber, green onion, cilantro, basil, and mint. Pour about ¼ cup (2 fl oz/60 ml) vinaigrette over the top and toss well. Taste and adjust with more vinaigrette, if necessary. Let stand for 5 minutes and then toss again. Garnish with the peanuts on top and serve. Pass the lime wedges at the table.

This dish proves that nutritious, low-fat turkey isn't just for Thanksgiving anymore. In this takeoff on the classic Italian veal saltimbocca, I put the prosciutto and sage in the sauce, giving it an incredible flavor boost. I recruit the kids to help flour the cutlets or gently pound thick cutlets.

turkey saltimbocca

Preheat the oven to 350°F (180°C). Put the flour in a shallow bowl. Season the cutlets on both sides with salt and pepper, and then coat both sides with the flour and tap off the excess. Place on a plate.

Heat a large ovenproof sauté pan over medium-high heat and add 1 tablespoon of the butter. When it begins to brown, add the oil and then add the cutlets. Cook, turning once, until golden on both sides, 3–4 minutes on each side. Transfer the pan to the oven to finish cooking, about 5 minutes. Transfer to a warmed platter.

Place the pan over medium-high heat and add 1 tablespoon of the butter. When the butter begins to brown, add the prosciutto and chopped sage and sauté until the prosciutto is puckered and golden, about 2 minutes. Add the wine, bring to a boil, stir, and boil for 1–2 minutes to reduce slightly. Swirl in the remaining 2 tablespoons butter off the heat and season to taste with salt and pepper. Spoon the sauce over the cutlets and serve right away.

½ cup (2½ oz/75 g) all-purpose flour

6 turkey cutlets, about ¼ lb (125 g) each and no more than ½-inch (1.5 cm) thick

kosher salt and freshly ground pepper

4 tablespoons (2 oz/60 g) unsalted butter

1 tablespoon extra-virgin olive oil

¼ lb (125 g) thinly sliced prosciutto, cut into narrow strips

2 tablespoons chopped fresh sage

½ cup (4 fl oz/125 ml) dry white wine

serves 4–6

These kebabs are perfect for family get-togethers. Imagine a platter piled high with juicy, smoke-kissed chicken skewers, accompanied by puffy Pita Pockets (page 26) and bowls of piquant Hummus (page 250) and Tabbouleh (page 150). Sounds like my kind of party. The yogurt keeps the chicken tender and carries the flavor of the cilantro, garlic, and green onion into the meat. Let the kids thread the chicken onto the skewers.

chicken kebabs

1½ lb (750 g) boneless, skinless chicken breasts or thighs, cut into 2-inch chunks

½ cup (4 oz/125 g) plain yogurt

½ cup (1½ oz/45 g) chopped green (spring) onion, including the tender green tops

1 large clove garlic, crushed

½ cup (¾ oz/20 g) chopped fresh cilantro (fresh coriander)

2 tablespoons extra-virgin olive oil

kosher salt and freshly ground pepper

1–2 medium zucchini, thickly sliced (optional)

1 cup (6 oz/185 g) cherry tomatoes (optional)

serves 4–6

In a large nonreactive bowl, combine the chicken, yogurt, green onion, garlic, cilantro, and oil and mix well. Season with 1 teaspoon salt and a few grinds of pepper. Cover and refrigerate for at least 3 hours or up to overnight.

Have ready 6 metal skewers or soak six 10-inch (25-cm) bamboo skewers in water to cover for at least 30 minutes. Prepare a medium-hot fire in a charcoal or gas grill. Make sure the grill rack is clean, then oil it and let the oil burn off for 5 minutes.

While the grill is warming up, divide the chicken chunks and zucchini and cherry tomatoes, if using, evenly among the skewers, and season lightly with salt and pepper. Place on the grill rack and grill, turning once, until the chicken is golden and opaque throughout but still juicy, about 8 minutes on each side. Serve right away.

"Finger" is a curious name for breaded chicken breast tenderloins. But that name has spawned a lucrative industry that turns out millions of frozen, packaged chicken fingers daily. I said no to those frozen digits years ago and instead make this tasty version at home using good-quality, organic chicken, which adults and kids alike can't seem to get enough of.

oven-fried chicken fingers

Preheat the oven to 425°F (220°C). Pour the oil into a rimmed baking sheet.

Place the flour, egg whites, and bread crumbs into 3 separate shallow bowls or pie pans and line them up, in that order. Season each bowl with 1 teaspoon salt and a few grinds of pepper. Stir the Parmesan, thyme, and parsley into the bread crumbs.

One at a time, dip the chicken pieces into the flour and tap off the excess, and then dip into the egg whites and allow the excess to drip off. Finally, roll in the bread crumbs and place on the prepared pan, spacing them 1–2 inches (2.5–5 cm) apart. (At this point, the chicken can be refrigerated, uncovered, for a few hours. The coating will dry out a bit, so it will crisp better in the oven.)

Bake for 8 minutes. Turn the pieces over and continue to bake until golden and opaque throughout, 8–10 minutes longer. Transfer to a platter and serve right away.

get creative

Dipping these tasty fingers into a delicious array of sauces makes them even more fun to eat, especially for the little ones. Choose from all kinds of savory concoctions, such as Tomato-Basil Sauce (page 235), Lemony Mayo (page 165), spicy mustard, or even good-quality BBQ sauce.

¼ cup (2 fl oz/60 ml) extra-virgin olive oil

½ cup (2½ oz/75 g) all-purpose (plain) flour

4 large egg whites, lightly beaten

1 cup (4 oz/125 g) plain dried bread crumbs

kosher salt and freshly ground pepper

½ cup (2 oz/60 g) grated Parmesan cheese

1 teaspoon chopped fresh thyme

1 tablespoon chopped fresh flat-leaf (Italian) parsley

3 boneless, skinless chicken breast halves, each cut into 4 strips, or 1¼ pounds (625 g) chicken tenders (about 12)

serves 4–6

Who can resist a mile-high cheeseburger, a thick porterhouse steak, a juicy marinated pork chop, or a succulent rack of lamb? No one at my house.

meat

When a juicy steak is sizzling on the grill, you can't keep me away from the fire. If a freshly made pork sausage is dancing in a sauté pan, I can't resist a taste. Wave a slow-smoked barbecued rib in front of my face and my knees go weak. I know that red meat has been getting a bad rap in recent years, but it isn't all bad. In fact, it is a good source of complete protein (important for muscle growth), iron, B vitamins, phosphorus, magnesium, and more. Occasionally, my husband throws a prime-cut steak on the grill, but you are more likely to see something with a bone—a thick-cut pork chop, short rib, rack of lamb, or rib steak—on our table. We all like to chew those bones long after the succulent meat is gone.

While my family doesn't eat meat every single day, we thoroughly enjoy it when we do. If you choose your cuts and who you buy them from wisely, and serve reasonable portions, meat is a very nutritious addition to your menu.

a family of meat eaters

My older daughter has liked beef, especially steak, for as long as I can remember. And she doesn't like it well done. It's medium-rare or nothing. Our whole family likes pork: slow-roasted shoulder, grilled chops, and griddled bacon, sausage, and ham. We like to think that we consume everything but the oink.

Years ago, we started a sheep-grazing program for our vineyards. The sheep mow the vineyards and produce lambs every spring. Every fall, we have lamb in our freezer waiting to be eaten, a delicious by-product of raising sheep.

We eat beef, pork, or lamb once or twice a week. My concern about how the animals are farmed and my family's health has helped me to make better choices when I do serve meat. We eat it less frequently than we once did, and when we do eat it, we make sure to know who the producer is and that it has been raised sustainably.

it's all in the cut

There are two types of cuts: tough and tender. Lamb and pork are often more tender than beef because the animals are smaller and slaughtered younger. Beef comes from a larger and older animal. A big steer not only yields more meat but also yields more cuts to suit specialized ways of cooking. Tough cuts need marinating or slow, moist heat, like braising, stewing, or slow roasting. Tender cuts need dry heat, like grilling, roasting, broiling, or sautéing.

shoulders and front legs

The front of the animal contains cuts that stand up to long, slow cooking. These include beef chuck, beef short ribs, lamb and pork shoulder, and veal and lamb shanks. They are also usually the least tender and the least expensive cuts on the animal, though their price has crept up over the years as consumers have discovered their amazing flavor and the ease of slow cooking. The meat is shot through with fat and collagen-rich connective tissue, which make it tough. Slow, moist cooking gradually leaches out the collagen and fat, which brings out the richness and flavor of the meat. The result? Meat so tender you can cut it with a fork. Recipes made with meat from the shoulders and front legs nearly always taste better reheated the next day.

the center

The center is divided into two parts, the rib (rack) and the loin. This is the prized real estate of the animal, yielding tender, rich meat marbled with fat. But it is also limited in size and quantity. The best-known center cuts are lamb rack, beef rib roasts, loin and tenderloin roasts, a variety of boneless steaks, and rib, sirloin, and T-bone steaks. Most of them are good candidates for roasting, grilling, broiling, or sautéing. Less-tender cuts, like flank steak and skirt steaks, are made tender by marinating and proper slicing. A few cuts in this section, including back and spare ribs and pork belly, benefit from braising.

rump and rear legs

The cuts from the rump and hind legs are more tender than the cuts from the front, but less tender than those from the center. Larger roasts, like leg of lamb and pork and beef top round, come from this part of the animal. They adapt well to moderate-heat roasting or braising. Smaller steak cuts are suitable for grilling, broiling, or sautéing and should be served medium or medium-rare. They are not as rich in fat and connective tissue as the shoulder, so overcooking will make them dry and tough.

ANTIBIOTICS AND HORMONES

Most of the antibiotics manufactured in the world go to livestock. Many of them are fed to cows, lambs, and hogs through their feed. That means the animal gets them whether it needs them or not. The animal isn't sick; the antibiotics are a preventive measure. Beef and lamb can receive growth hormones during feedlot finishing, but they must be withdrawn a specified amount of time before slaughter to prevent them from entering the meat. Pigs do not receive growth hormones. Their breeding and nutrition are so streamlined and efficient, they achieve slaughter size within six months.

the other cut: ground meat

Ground beef can come from the chuck,
sirloin, and short plate, as well as from
trimmings from other parts. Fat is
ground into the meat, up to 30 percent,
to lend moistness and flavor. Ground
beef labeled lean and extra lean have
less added fat. Some restaurants
have secret recipes for their hamburger
meat, carefully selecting different
cuts and fat content to make the
ultimate burger.

Ground pork and lamb usually come
from the shoulder and neck, with the
shoulder's natural fat content adding
flavor and moistness. Additional fat
from other parts of the animal can
be ground into the meat for sausage.

seasonality and buying

Beef, pork, and lamb are available
year-round. In the past, the slaughter
of animals was seasonal, with both
the breeding patterns and the amount
of pasture available to support them
influencing when the slaughter was
held. For example, sheep were bred in
the fall and lambed in the spring when
grass was abundant enough to support
nursing ewes. Today, the season for
spring lamb extends from March to
October, and most shoppers consider
these youngsters the best buy because
they are slaughtered at a younger age.

I often buy live animals raised by local
farmers and split a whole steer or
hog with one or more other families.
These animals are usually raised
according to organic standards without

the certification, and because I know
the farmers, I feel comfortable buying
from them. We have the animals
dispatched at the local abattoir, where
federal inspection is not necessary
because the meat is not being sold
to the public. If you decide to go this
route, you will need a lot of freezer
space because the butchered animal
is delivered all at once. If buying whole
animals is not for you, go online to
look for local farmers who sell their
meat to nearby grocery stores and
farmers' markets. Some will even ship
directly to you.

When buying meat, select prime,
choice, or select beef and prime or
choice lamb. Meat is graded on its
quality and on the amount of marbling
(the more marbling, the more tender
the meat). Lamb and beef without
grades, usually sold as store brand
meats, are of lesser quality, which is
reflected in their price. Because hogs
are slaughtered at such a young age
and are highly uniform, pork is not
graded, but it is government inspected.

Beef and lamb should be a rich red with
no sign of discoloration. Pork should
be a pale, uniform pink. Reject any
meat that has an off odor. Choose
tightly wrapped, undamaged packages
and keep them cold for the journey
home, popping them into a cooler if
you plan to run more errands. Once
you are home, leave the meat in the
store packaging until you are ready
to use it, store it in the coldest part
of the refrigerator, and then use it
within three days.

CONVENTIONAL, NATURAL, GRASS FED, AND ORGANIC: WHAT ARE THE DIFFERENCES?

- **Conventional:** No USDA definition. Hormones and subtherapeutic and therapeutic antibiotics are used in production. Feed and pasture are grown with chemical pesticides and fertilizer. Grazing is not allowed during the finishing period, which lasts about six months.

- **Natural:** The USDA definition specifies "no artificial ingredients and minimally processed." Labels may claim no hormones or antibiotics have been used, but this has not been checked by an independent party. No restrictions on use of chemical pesticides and fertilizer for feed and pasture, and no standards for grazing.

- **Grass fed:** No USDA definition. Grass fed is verified by affidavit from the producer, not an independent inspection. There is no third-party checking for hormones or antibiotics and no restrictions on use of chemical pesticides for feed and pasture.

- **Organic:** Must follow USDA National Organic Standards. The use of hormones and antibiotics is prohibited. Feed and pasture must be 100 percent organically grown. Outdoor access is required for cattle, weather permitting. The nutritional/behavioral needs of each species are taken into consideration when determining requirements. Cattle can be grain finished for three months. Some organic meats also carry the Certified Humane and Animal Welfare Approved label, which prohibits the use of hormones and antibiotics in livestock and promotes sustainable production. It is third-party certified but is not recognized by the USDA.

There's nothing like the sizzle, pop, and aroma of steaks, hearty lamb kebabs, or garlicky pork chops being grilled over an open fire. In addition to smoky flavor, it adds a rustic festivity to your meal.

dry-cured bacon

Fat is flavor, and this dry-cured bacon has plenty of both! Rub some salt and brown sugar on a pork belly and three days later you will wake up to bacon. The cut, which comes from the back and sides (belly) of a hog, is salted and lightly dried, not smoked, and is reminiscent of an Italian pancetta. Traditional American bacon is made from pork belly and smoked.

I use a dry cure, which is easier than a wet cure because you don't have to deal with sloshing containers of brine. The bacon comes out nicely salted with a hint of sweetness, and because it is not smoked, the delicate pork flavor shines through. It can be used as you would store-bought smoked bacon: in salads and sandwiches, alongside eggs, or in any recipe that would benefit from a shot of bacon flavor.

bacon flavor variations

Because of its fat, bacon can easily take on flavors from the far corners of the world. For a flavorful ethnic spin on the basic bacon recipe on page 206, add the following spices to the dry rub.

Asian bacon

- 2 teaspoons Chinese 5-spice powder
- 4 large garlic cloves, pressed

Use this bacon chopped in fried rice recipes, stir-fried with long beans, or wrapped around water chestnuts and roasted until the bacon is crisp.

Mediterranean bacon

- 1½ teaspoons ground fennel seed
- 1 teaspoon red chile flakes

Add this fragrant chopped bacon to tomato and meat ragus or white bean and vegetable soups, or use it to top pizzas.

Alsatian bacon

- 1½ teaspoons coarsely ground caraway seeds
- 2 teaspoons cracked black pepper

Use thickly chopped bacon in choucroute, the famous dish of Alsace, or add to braised pork and sauerkraut. Add crisp-cooked, chopped bacon to vinegary potato salad or to a simple cheese quiche.

what you'll need to cure bacon

- small bowl and spoon
- ½ cup (2½ oz/75 g) kosher salt
- ¼ cup (2 oz/60 g) firmly packed brown sugar
- 2–2½-lb (1–1.25-kg) piece skinless pork belly (about one-third whole belly), 1¼–1½ inches (3–4 cm) thick
- cutting board
- coarsely ground pepper (optional)
- 2-gal (8-l) resealable plastic bag
- nonreactive baking dish
- large wire rack

1 make the brine

In the small bowl, stir together the salt and sugar until well mixed. Place the pork belly on the cutting board.

2 rub the brine on

Sprinkle pepper over the fat side of the meat until well covered, if desired. Then thoroughly rub one-fourth of the salt-sugar mixture into the fat side, and the remaining three-fourths of the mixture into the meat side.

3 let the belly brine

Slip the belly into the plastic bag, press out the air, seal closed, and place in the baking dish. Put the dish in the refrigerator. Turn the bag over once each day for 3 days. The juice will leach out of the meat into the bag. Do not drain the juices off.

4 rinse and dry

On the third day, remove the belly from the bag, rinse it briefly under cold running water, and pat it dry. Put the wire rack in the baking dish, put the belly on the rack, and place the dish, uncovered, in the refrigerator to dry for 2 hours.

5 taste it and store it

Cut a slice, fry it, and taste it. If you prefer it saltier, cure the bacon a day longer the next time. If you prefer less salt, rinse off the rub a day earlier. Wrap well and refrigerate for up to 1 week. Or slice the bacon, wrap in parchment (baking) paper, then plastic wrap, and freeze for up to 3 months.

Each summer, when tomatoes are bursting with juiciness, everyone in our house looks forward to a good BLT—but with avocados (making it a BLTA). Instead of using slices of avocado, which slip out of the sandwich too easily, I mix the avocados with the mayonnaise. Another tip: Make the bacon the top layer. It provides traction that keeps the bread slices from sliding around.

the best BLTA sandwich

for the avo-mayo

2 avocados, peeled, pitted, and coarsely mashed

3 tablespoons mayonnaise, store-bought or Lemony Mayo (page 165)

1 teaspoon finely chopped fresh tarragon

¼ teaspoon lemon juice

kosher salt and freshly ground pepper

12 slices bacon (page 204), ⅛ inch (3 mm) thick

8 slices white or whole wheat (wholemeal) bread, lightly toasted

8–12 ripe tomato slices

kosher salt and freshly ground black pepper

8 small butter (Boston) lettuce leaves

makes 4 sandwiches

To make the avo-mayo, in a small bowl, combine the avocados, mayonnaise, tarragon, and lemon juice and mix well. Season to taste with salt and pepper.

To make the sandwiches, heat a large sauté pan over medium heat. Add the bacon and sauté until most of its fat is rendered and the bacon is crisp on the edges but still chewy at the center, about 5 minutes. Transfer to paper towels to drain, then cut each slice in half crosswise and keep warm.

Line up 4 of the toasted bread slices on a work surface and slather each slice thickly with the avo-mayo. Top each with tomato slices, covering the mayo. Season with salt and pepper. Top with the lettuce leaves and then the bacon, dividing evenly.

Spread the remaining 4 bread slices with avocado mayo. Place mayo side down on the bacon and press down firmly to lock everything into place. Cut in half and serve right away.

One summer, my garden yielded a bumper crop of peppers and chiles, in all colors, shapes, and sizes. I had already grilled, peeled, and marinated mountains of the harvest, and then I suddenly had an idea: when life gives you too many peppers, have a fajita party. If you or your kids shy away from chile heat, use all bell peppers.

steak fajitas

Thinly slice the steak with the grain, and place in a nonreactive bowl. Add the lime juice, garlic, chopped cilantro, and 1 tablespoon of the oil and mix well. Cover and refrigerate for 1–2 hours.

Seed and stem the bell peppers and pasilla and Anaheim chiles, trim away the ribs, and cut lengthwise into strips ½ inch (12 mm) wide. Place in a bowl, add the onion wedges, 1 tablespoon of the oil, and some salt, and toss to coat evenly.

Heat a large sauté pan over high heat. When the pan is hot, add the peppers, chiles, and onions and stir quickly to blister the skins of the peppers and chiles. Cook until they are tender-crisp and the skins are flecked with black spots, about 4 minutes, reducing the heat if the pan begins smoking too much. Turn the mixture out onto a serving plate.

Brush most of the marinade from the meat strips and season with salt. Return the pan to high heat. When it is hot, add 1 tablespoon of the oil, allow it to heat, and add half of the steak. Let the meat sear and brown on the underside, 2–3 minutes, and then quickly stir to cook on all sides, about 2 minutes longer. Pour the meat on top of the peppers and repeat with the other half of the steak and the remaining 1 tablespoon oil. Add to the platter.

Top with the cilantro leaves and ring the plate with the lime wedges. Serve right away with the tortillas.

1 lb (500 g) well-trimmed skirt steak

2 tablespoons lime juice

3 cloves garlic, pressed

3 tablespoons chopped fresh cilantro (fresh coriander), plus extra leaves for garnish

4 tablespoons (2 fl oz/ 60 ml) extra-virgin olive oil

1 *each* small red and yellow bell pepper (capsicum), pasilla chile, and Anaheim chile

1 cup (4 oz/125 g) thin onion wedges

kosher salt

8 lime wedges

flour tortillas, homemade (page 281) or store-bought, warmed

serves 1 6

In the days before I knew better, I made beef stew with chuck. It is very flavorful, of course, but if you cook it a long time, it begins to dry out. So, I switched to boneless short ribs, which always stay really nice and moist. My daughters like to sop up the juices of this hearty, delicious stew with thick slices of crusty bread.

braised beef stew

1½ lb (750 g) boneless beef short ribs, each 2–3 inches (5–7.5 cm) long

kosher salt and freshly ground pepper

1 tablespoon extra-virgin olive oil

1 yellow onion, diced

2 carrots, peeled and cut into 1-inch (2.5-cm) chunks

1 parsnip, peeled and cut into 1-inch (2.5-cm) chunks

2 large cloves garlic

6 oz (185 g) small white or cremini mushrooms, trimmed and halved

1 cup (8 fl oz/250 ml) dry red wine

1 cup (6 oz/185 g) fresh or canned diced tomatoes with their juice

1 bay leaf

1 teaspoon chopped fresh thyme

serves 4–6

Preheat the oven to 350°F (180°C). Cut each short rib in half crosswise. Season the meat well with salt and pepper.

Heat a Dutch oven or similar heavy pot with a tight lid over medium-high heat and add the oil. When the oil is hot, add the beef and sear on all sides until well browned, about 8 minutes.

Add the onion, carrots, parsnip, garlic, and mushrooms and cook, stirring often, until the vegetables are lightly colored, about 5 minutes. Add the wine, bring to a boil, and cook for 5 minutes to reduce slightly. Add the tomatoes, bay leaf, and thyme and return to a boil. Cover tightly, transfer to the oven, and cook until the meat is tender when pierced with a fork, about 1½ hours.

Taste and adjust the seasoning with salt and pepper. Serve directly from the pot.

I love T-bone pork chops—also called bone-in center-cut chops—because you get both a little of the loin and a little of the tenderloin. Juicy and aromatic, these Asian-inspired chops go surprisingly well with applesauce. Don't worry if your kids declare them too exotic before they try them. After just one taste, they'll be back for more.

grilled 5-spice pork chops

Place the pork chops in a nonreactive dish. In a small bowl, stir together the ginger, garlic, 5-spice powder, oil, and a few grinds of coarsely ground pepper. Rub the ginger mixture evenly over both sides of the chops, cover, and refrigerate for at least 1 hour or up to overnight.

Prepare a medium-hot fire in a charcoal or gas grill. Make sure the grill rack is clean, then oil it and let the oil burn off for 5 minutes.

Season the pork chops on both sides with salt. Place on the grill rack and grill, turning once, until etched with grill marks, golden, and light pink at the center when cut into with a knife, 6–7 minutes on each side. Transfer to a warmed platter and let rest for 5 minutes before serving. Pass the applesauce at the table.

4–6 T-bone pork chops, each about ¾ inch (2 cm) thick

2 teaspoons peeled and minced fresh ginger

2 large cloves garlic, pressed

1 teaspoon Chinese 5-spice powder

1 tablespoon extra-virgin olive oil

kosher salt and freshly ground pepper

vegetable oil for the grill

chunky applesauce, homemade (page 109) or store-bought, for serving

serves 4–6

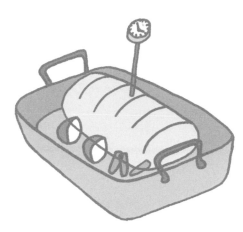

The marinade on this roast is about as simple as one can get, and it tastes magnificent. Have the kids roughly strip the herb leaves from the big stems—don't bother to remove the small stems—and then crush the herbs in their hands to release the essential oils before tossing them into the bowl.

roasted pork tenderloin

1½ lb (750 g) pork tenderloin (1 large or 2 small), trimmed of fat and sinew

4 large cloves garlic, pressed

2 tablespoons fresh rosemary leaves

3 tablespoons fresh thyme leaves

2 tablespoons extra-virgin olive oil

kosher salt and freshly ground pepper

serves 4–6

Place the pork in a nonreactive dish. In a bowl, stir together the herbs, garlic, 1 tablespoon of the oil, and some pepper, then rub evenly over the pork. Cover and refrigerate for at least 2 hours or up to overnight.

Preheat the oven to 400°F (200°C). Remove the pork from the marinade and brush off most of the garlic and herbs. Season the pork with salt. The pepper from the marinade should be enough. Heat a large ovenproof sauté pan over medium-high heat and add the remaining oil. When the oil is hot, add the pork (if it is too long for the pan, you can bend it to fit), and sear on all sides until golden brown, 7–10 minutes, reducing the heat slightly if the pan gets too smoky.

Transfer to the oven and roast until the center is light pink when cut into at the thickest part with a knife, or an instant-read thermometer inserted in the thickest part registers 140°F (60°C), about 20 minutes.

Transfer the pork to a cutting board and let rest for 10 minutes, then slice and serve right away.

get creative

The tenderloin can also be grilled. Prepare a hot fire for indirect grilling. Sear the pork on all sides directly over the fire, and then move it to the cooler area, cover the grill, and cook for 15–20 minutes. It's delicious with the Roasted Plums (page 119)—minus the whipped crème fraîche.

These meatballs are easy to make, with just one caveat: don't squish the ingredients together roughly. Be gentle and you will be rewarded with delicate, flavorful meatballs. You can also roll them very small, an inch (2.5 cm) or so in diameter—a size that kids love.

best-ever meatballs

In a small bowl, mix together the bread crumbs and milk and let soak for 10 minutes. Drain in a fine-mesh sieve, pressing out the excess milk. Discard the milk.

In a large bowl, combine the meats and mix lightly. In a separate bowl, combine the soaked bread crumbs, egg, garlic, shallot, fennel, parsley, and cheese. Mix until evenly combined.

Add the bread crumb mixture to the meat mixture, sprinkle with 2 teaspoons salt, and then top with some pepper. Quickly and gently mix with your hands to combine the ingredients evenly, but avoid over-mixing, which can make the meatballs tough.

Preheat the oven to 425°F (220°C). Drizzle the oil evenly over the bottom of a large rimmed baking sheet.

Use a 1–fl oz (30-ml) ice cream scoop to portion the meat mixture into 16 mounds, spacing them well apart on the prepared pan. Pick up each mound, gently roll it into a ball, and return it to the pan.

Bake the meatballs for 15 minutes. Roll them over and continue to bake until browned and cooked through, about 15 minutes longer.

Meanwhile, bring the tomato sauce to a simmer. When the meatballs are ready, transfer them to the sauce and simmer for 45 minutes to finish. Serve over pasta or tuck into crusty bread for sandwiches.

1 cup (4 oz/125 g) plain dried bread crumbs

½ cup (4 fl oz/125 ml) whole milk

½ lb (250 g) *each* ground (minced) beef and veal

¼ lb (125 g) ground (minced) pork

1 large egg, lightly beaten

2 cloves garlic, pressed

1 tablespoon minced shallot

¼ teaspoon ground fennel

1 tablespoon chopped fresh flat-leaf (Italian) parsley

¼ cup (1 oz/30 g) grated Parmesan cheese

kosher salt and freshly ground pepper

2 tablespoons olive oil

Tomato-Basil Sauce (page 235)

serves 4–6

Growing up, I overheard plenty of serious adult meatball conversation around the dinner table: whose meatballs were heavy, whose fell apart, whose were too spicy, whose were bland, and on and on. If a male relative announced his engagement, the first question anyone asked about his future wife was, "Can she make a good meatball?"

Then someone would utter Nana DiGregorio's name and a hush would fall over the table. Nana's meatballs were revered, especially the little veal ones she made for a soup that included nothing more than the meatballs, broth, chopped parsley, and a sprinkle of Parmesan. These jewels were the meatballs to which every other meatball was compared. They were light, flavorful, and delicate: so light they halved at the slightest touch of a spoon; so flavorful you couldn't describe the parts, only the whole; so delicate they would collapse if bigger than the size of a large olive.

I have yet to duplicate Nana's meatballs, but if you make the recipe on page 217 with ground veal only and make the balls small, they would be very close. Kids especially like their size and light texture. Float them in soup, using a good, rich chicken broth if you don't want to make veal broth.

These kebabs are just another form of meatball—like having a lamb burger on a stick. My kids gravitate toward anything cooked on a skewer, so I present them at the table on the skewers, and then slide them off so no one gets poked. Or, you can shape the mixture into patties, grill them, and serve tucked into a pita.

lamb kebabs with pita

¾ cup (4½ oz/140 g) minced yellow onion

3 cloves garlic, pressed

2 tablespoons chopped fresh cilantro (fresh coriander)

1 tablespoon chopped fresh mint

1 tablespoon chopped fresh flat-leaf (Italian) parsley

1½ lb (750 g) ground (minced) lamb shoulder

1 teaspoon ground cumin

1½ teaspoons kosher salt

freshly ground pepper

vegetable oil for grill rack

pita breads, homemade (page 26) or store-bought

Cool-as-a-Cucumber Raita (page 65) or plain yogurt

serves 4–6

Have ready 3 flat metal skewers, or soak four 10-inch (25-cm) bamboo skewers in water to cover for at least 30 minutes.

In a large bowl, combine the onion, garlic, cilantro, mint, and parsley and mix well. Add the lamb and sprinkle with the cumin, salt, and a few grinds of pepper. Quickly and gently mix with your hands to combine all of the ingredients evenly.

Divide the mixture into 12 equal portions, and shape each portion into ovals. Drain the bamboo skewers, if using. Pick up a patty, stick the skewer lengthwise down the center, then repack the meat in the same shape around the skewer. Repeat, threading on 2 more ovals if using a bamboo skewer or 3 more ovals if using a metal skewer and spacing the ovals ½ inch (12 mm) apart. Place the skewer on a flat tray. Repeat until you have filled all of the skewers. Refrigerate for 20 minutes to firm up the meat before grilling.

Prepare a medium-hot fire in a charcoal or gas grill. Make sure the grill rack is clean, then oil it and let the oil burn off for 5 minutes.

Season the kebabs lightly with salt and pepper. Place on the grill rack and grill, turning once, until golden on the outside and cooked through but still juicy, about 10 minutes on each side. Transfer the skewers to a serving plate and let rest for 5 minutes. Then slide the kebabs off the skewers and serve right away with the pita and raita.

Creamy hummus, coconut-laced rice pudding, spicy chickpea curry—who says beans and grains are boring?

pasta, grains & legumes

Almost no one would turn away from a big, steaming bowl of pasta tossed with fresh tomato-basil sauce. Pure comfort food, kids and grown-ups alike dig right in. But folks seldom swoon when a plate of refried beans or a hearty lentil stew is put on the table, and grains have long carried even less attraction. Times are changing, though, and people's opinions are changing with them. Beans and grains are now being championed as nutritional powerhouses, loaded with protein, fiber, vitamins, minerals, and carbohydrates, and cooks are coming up with delectable ways to serve them. They are also discovering how practical these ingredients are: they keep for a long time in the pantry and can easily be turned into a delicious dish.

The great thing about these staples is that you can pull them from the pantry at a moment's notice, and with only a handful of other ingredients, prepare a hearty, deliciously textured meal that is packed with flavor.

an easy choice

I am amazed at how much pasta, grains, and beans we incorporate into the meals at our house. I always think we are a little light in this department, and then I open the doors to the pantry. It is stuffed with a huge variety of rice, beans, lentils, and pasta of all shapes and sizes. Every time I grab a bag of rice or beans, I realize how easy it is to turn them into a satisfying meal. You sometimes have to plan ahead, soaking beans overnight or putting whole grains on to boil earlier than their refined counterparts, but that's not difficult. And pasta, whether whole grain or not, is always a breeze.

what's in a dough?

The best dried pasta is made from high-protein semolina flour, milled from durum wheat. Because it is high in protein, it produces a smooth, shiny dough that dries quickly and holds its shape. Fresh pasta, which usually includes eggs, is sometimes made from semolina flour, but is more often made from all-purpose (plain) flour. Whole wheat (wholemeal) pastas, dried and fresh, are made with whole wheat semolina flour or semolina flour with bran added. These latter pastas deliver the benefit of fiber, but offer nearly the same nutritional benefits as pasta made from refined wheat. You can also find pasta made from farro, quinoa, corn, and rice.

how much should I serve?

The recommended serving size for pasta is ½ cup (3 oz/90 g) cooked, even though most packages list double that amount. This is a disappointment to anyone who likes pasta—and that's just about everyone. If you want to decide for yourself how much to cook, use these measures: ½ cup (2 oz/60 g) dried pasta shapes yields 1 cup (5 oz/155 g) cooked; 2 oz strand pasta yields 1 cup cooked; or 2 oz dried egg noodles yield just over ½ cup cooked.

DRIED PASTA SHAPES PUT TO GOOD USE

- Pasta for soup: *stelline, acini di pepe, anellini,* alphabet, *tubettini,* orzo

- Pasta for salads: farfalle, *gemelli,* fusilli, macaroni

- Pasta for brothy, marinara, or light cream sauces: capellini, vermicelli, linguine, tagliatelle

- Pasta for meat, heavier cream, or chunky sauces: *cavatelli,* orecchiette, spaghetti, fettuccine, *pappardelle, bucatini,* penne

- Pasta for baked dishes: ziti, macaroni, lasagna, rigatoni, penne, *cavatappi*

- Pasta to stuff: *conchiglie,* manicotti, *lumache*

the world of grains

Grains can turn up in every meal of the day, from your morning cereal bowl to your lunchtime soup bowl to your supper risotto bowl. They come both whole and refined and in a variety of shapes and sizes. The most popular grains are rice, corn, wheat, oats, and barley, with quinoa, millet, and rye slowly beginning to gain a following.

Whole grains are colorful, varied, and more nutritionally beneficial than their refined relatives. Think brown rice versus white rice. A critical component of a healthy diet, whole grains are low in fat and are a good source of complex carbohydrates, fiber, vitamins, and minerals. They are also rich in lignans, antioxidants, phenolic acids, and phytochemicals, which are thought to reduce the risk of heart disease, cancer, and diabetes. That's pretty powerful stuff.

Refined grains seem pale and uniform by comparison. Most have some or all of their bran and germ removed by milling, pearling, or polishing, processes that allow them to cook faster. Some refined grains are enriched with vitamins and minerals after processing, but the loss of fiber is permanent. Whole grains aren't always the best choice, however. Risotto would lack its creaminess if the rice bran were still intact. Aromatic rices such as basmati and jasmine are more fragrant in their refined state. Degerminated cornmeal makes corn bread with a sweeter taste and finer texture. Lightly processed oats turn out a faster breakfast porridge. In other words, it is important to balance your consumption of whole and refined grains.

HOW TO COOK PERFECT PASTA

1 Use at least 4 quarts (4 l) water to cook 1 pound (500 g) pasta and bring it to a rolling boil.

2 Always salt the cooking water, using about 2 tablespoons for each pound (500 g) of pasta. Never add oil. If the pasta sticks together, you can loosen it with a little sauce.

3 Add the pasta all at once and stir immediately to prevent it from sticking together.

4 Cook until al dente—in other words, tender but firm to the bite. Use the cooking time on the package as a guide, but begin checking a couple of minutes in advance.

5 Drain the pasta the moment it tests done. Save a little of the cooking water in case you need extra moisture to extend the sauce.

Common brown lentils, split peas, and chickpeas (garbanzo beans) were winter staples on the dinner circuit at our house when I was a child. The first time I tried green French lentils, I knew I had found something to add to my kitchen cupboard. The brown lentils of my youth paled in comparison to the pert-textured Gallic variety. When I ate my first exotically spiced dal at an Indian restaurant in San Francisco, I swore I was eating yellow split peas. The ever-patient hostess explained that they were lentils, red lentils at that, and then had the chef show me what they looked like raw. What culinary alchemy, I wondered, turned those bright red legumes a curious yellow.

Unfortunately, chickpeas and split peas have remained immutable. But I did discover yellow split peas, which added color to my life. And on a cold winter night, I still like a good split pea soup made with a ham hock or a hearty chickpea stew. I also know that legumes will always be on my dinner table because of their satisfying meatiness and the way they soak up other flavors. The fact that they harbor so much nutrition is just icing on the cake.

buying and preparing beans

Dried beans come in a myriad of sizes and colors. Buy a few different varieties and experiment. Old beans take longer

A LIST OF WHOLE AND REFINED GRAINS

- Corn: popcorn, cornmeal, grits, polenta
- Wheat: farro, spelt, cracked wheat, bulgur
- Rice: wild, brown, white aromatic; long, medium, and short grain enriched
- Oats: whole, cracked, and whole rolled, rolled quick cooking and instant
- Barley: hulled, pearled
- Rye: dark, light
- Millet
- Quinoa

beans and lentils

Once you start eating grains, you can step up to the plate and add more fiber and vitamins to your diet by pairing them with dried beans, peas, or lentils, all of which are in the legume family. Legumes are low in fat and high in fiber, folate, potassium, iron, and magnesium. When you slap together a bean and a grain, you have created a complete protein without a trace of cholesterol. It is a perfect and healthful substitute for meat.

Beans, lentils, and peas come in a wild array of textures and a rainbow of colors. I like to line them up in clear glass jars on my shelves so I can admire them. Some of my favorite beans out of the hundreds available are kidney, pinto, cranberry, cannellini, and black.

to cook, so purchase them at a store that has a pretty high turnover or straight from the farmer. Look for shiny, whole plump beans that are uniform in size. If you buy them in bags, pass up packages that contain broken beans or a layer of silt in the bottom.

Lentils, like beans, come in a wide range of colors and should be plump and whole. The exception is split lentils, which have had their outer hull removed. The disks should be round and smooth and free of dust and silt. Look for the same qualities in split peas, both green and yellow, as you do in split lentils.

When you prepare beans, lentils, or peas, always begin by pouring them onto a flat surface, such as a cutting board or baking pan, and picking out any wrinkled beans or stones. Then pour them into a sieve and rinse them well under running cold water until the water runs clear. Most recipes call for soaking beans overnight in water to cover at cool room temperature or in the refrigerator. You don't need to soak lentils or peas, however.

fresh pasta

Fresh pasta dough turns the task of making a favorite dinner into a fun activity for the whole family. We eat fresh pasta once or twice a week. I pull pasta dough from the refrigerator and put it on the counter to warm up before rolling. When my daughters discover it sitting there, the fight begins over who gets to roll it out.

While my daughters think rolling out the dough is fun, I find it cathartic. I love the feel of the smooth, shiny dough as it passes over my hand, through the machine, and out the bottom, just a little bit thinner each time. It is gratifying to see the pile of finished pasta getting higher and higher as the rolled dough is cut into ribbons. You can roll quite a bit in a very short time, and once it is rolled and cut, it cooks in a flash.

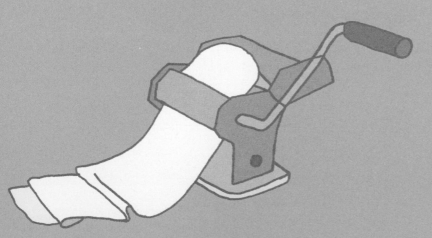

fresh ribbon pasta

Fresh pasta dough is easily cut into varying thicknesses with either a machine cutter or by hand. The following ribbon pastas are listed from the thinnest to thickest width. Spaghetti cut by machine or hand will be slightly square, not round, in shape.

As a rule of thumb, thinner pastas are more suited to light and delicate sauces, while thicker pastas can stand up to rich, meaty sauces.

spaghetti: $\frac{1}{16}$ inch (.15 cm) thick

linguine: $\frac{1}{8}$ inch (.3 cm) thick

tagliatelle: $\frac{3}{16}$ inch (.5 cm) thick

fettucine: $\frac{1}{4}$ inch (.6 cm) thick

pappardelle: 1 inch (2.5 cm) thick

to cut with a machine

Attach the appropriate cutter to your pasta machine, and feed the pasta sheet through the cutter according to the manufacturer's directions.

to cut by hand

If your pasta machine does not come with cutters for all widths, cut your pasta sheets into 12-inch (30-cm) lengths, dust with flour or semolina, and roll tightly. Use a knife to cut to the desired width and then unroll the pasta, shake and dust with flour, and lay on a tray.

once the pasta is cut

Lay the cut pasta on a rimmed baking sheet dusted with flour. Pasta can be cooked immediately or allowed to air dry, uncovered, for up to 2 hours.

what you'll need to make fresh pasta

- a large bowl and a small bowl
- wooden spoon
- 1 cup (5 oz/155 g) all-purpose (plain) flour
- 1 cup (5 oz/155 g) semolina flour
- 1½ teaspoons kosher salt
- whisk
- 2 large eggs
- 1 tablespoon plus 2 teaspoons cold water
- 1 tablespoon extra-virgin olive oil
- plastic wrap
- rolling pin
- hand-cranked pasta machine

1 prep the ingredients

In the large bowl, using the spoon, stir together both flours and the salt. In the small bowl, whisk together the eggs, water, and oil.

2 mix it up

Make a well in the flour and add the egg mixture to it. Using the spoon, mix the dry ingredients with the wet ingredients until combined.

3 knead the dough

Lightly flour a work surface, and turn the dough out onto it. Knead until smooth and elastic—like stiff Play-Doh—about 5 minutes. If the dough is too dry, add drops of water, a few at a time. If too wet, add flour, a big pinch at a time.

4 make dough disks

Cut the dough into thirds, and flatten each piece into disks ½ inch (12 mm) thick. Wrap in plastic wrap and let rest for 45 minutes at room temperature or overnight in the refrigerator. If the dough has been chilled, bring it to room temperature (about 20 minutes) before rolling.

5 roll out the pasta

Using the rolling pin, roll the dough disk ¼ inch (6 mm) thick. Adjust the rollers of the pasta machine to the widest setting. Run 1 piece of the dough through the rollers 3 times, folding the dough in half each time, and flouring it lightly if it begins to stick. Wrap in plastic wrap and let rest for 15 minutes.

6 keep on rollin'

Adjust the rollers to the next narrowest setting and feed the dough through each progressively narrower setting until you have a long, thin, smooth sheet and the dough has run through the narrowest setting. Dust lightly with flour if the dough becomes sticky. It should be thin enough to see your hand through it.

7 set aside

Dust the pasta sheet lightly with flour, fold into thirds, and wrap in plastic wrap. Leave at room temperature until ready to use, up to 30 minutes, or refrigerate up to overnight. Repeat with the remaining dough.

ricotta and herb ravioli

semolina flour for dusting

3 cups (1½ lb/750 g) fresh ricotta cheese, homemade (page 52) or store-bought

½ cup (2 oz/60 g) grated Parmesan

I large egg, lightly beaten

I tablespoon chopped fresh flat-leaf (Italian) parsley

kosher salt and freshly ground pepper

I lb (500 g) fresh pasta dough, in sheets (page 228)

4 cups (32 fl oz/1 l) Tomato-Basil Sauce (page 235) or store-bought tomato sauce

makes about sixty 2-inch (5-cm) square ravioli; serves 4–6

Dust 2 rimmed baking sheets with semolina flour. In a bowl, stir together both cheeses, the egg, and the parsley. Add I teaspoon salt and a few grinds of pepper and mix well.

Lightly flour a work surface and lay a pasta sheet on it. Dot the sheet with evenly spaced heaping teaspoons of the cheese mixture, spacing them 1½ inches (4 cm) apart. Using your fingertip, dampen the edges of the sheet and the spaces between the mounds with water. Lay a second pasta sheet of the same size on top. Starting at the edge of the filling, press outward from each mound to remove any trapped air and seal the pasta. Using a sharp knife, cut the ravioli into 2-inch (5-cm) squares, trimming away any ragged edges.

Place the ravioli on the prepared pan. Cover with a dish towel and repeat with the remaining filling and pasta sheets. Pasta scraps can be saved and cooked separately or discarded. Uncooked ravioli can be frozen directly on the pan. Once frozen, transfer them to zippered plastic bags and use within 3 months.

Fill a large pot three-fourths full of water and place over high heat. When it comes to a boil, add 2 tablespoons salt. Carefully drop half of the ravioli into the boiling water. When the water returns to a boil, reduce the heat to medium and simmer until tender, about 2 minutes. Using a skimmer, transfer to a warmed large, shallow bowl and spoon about I cup (8 fl oz/250 ml) of the sauce over the top. Keep warm. Cook the remaining ravioli the same way and add to the bowl. Spoon the remaining sauce over the top, toss gently, and serve right away.

get creative

For spinach-ricotta ravioli, add ½ cup (3½ oz/110 g) cooked, finely chopped spinach to the cheese filling.

Our tomato plants are healthy bearers, so in the summer and fall, we purée the excess tomatoes and strain and freeze the purée, ensuring us a taste of summer throughout the winter. I man the blender, and the kids handle the straining—teamwork that gets a mountain of tomatoes done in a flash. If you don't have fresh, ripe tomatoes, substitute 3 cans (45 oz/1.25 kg) of organic diced tomatoes.

fresh tomato and basil pasta

To make the sauce, put the oil and garlic in a large saucepan. Turn the heat to medium and cook until the garlic is golden on all sides, about 4 minutes. Remove from the heat.

Core and quarter the tomatoes. Working in batches, purée the tomatoes in a blender until smooth, and then strain through a coarse-mesh sieve into the pan with the oil and garlic. Add the bay leaf, sugar, 1 teaspoon salt, and a few grinds of pepper. Place over medium-high heat and bring to a boil. Reduce the heat to low and simmer, uncovered, until thickened, about 45 minutes.

Just before the sauce is ready, bring a large pot three-fourths full of salted water to a boil, add the spaghetti, and cook until al dente, according to package directions.

Stir the basil into the sauce and simmer for 5 minutes. Taste and adjust the seasoning with salt and pepper. Drain the pasta. Spoon about ¾ cup (6 fl oz/180 ml) of the sauce into the bottom of a warmed serving bowl. Add the pasta and toss to coat. Ladle more sauce over the top, sprinkle with Parmesan, and serve right away.

get creative

Serve this dish with meatballs (page 217) or make it a heartier meal with the addition of sautéed mushrooms; cooked, crumbled sausage; or leftover shredded braised beef or pork.

for the tomato-basil sauce

3 tablespoons extra-virgin olive oil

5 large cloves garlic

3 lb (1.5 kg) fresh plum (Roma) tomatoes

1 bay leaf

2 teaspoons sugar

kosher salt and freshly ground black pepper

½ cup (1 oz/30 g) firmly packed torn fresh basil leaves

¾ lb (375 g) spaghetti or other strand pasta

grated Parmesan cheese for serving

serves 4–6

When my daughters were small, they preferred organic mac and cheese from a box, with its powdered "cheese" product, over my homemade mac and cheese, with its cave-aged Gruyère and Parmesan. I was horrified. So I banned the boxed stuff for a few months, it faded from memory, and then I introduced this recipe. They liked it at once. We train our kids to eat what they eat; we can un-train them, too. I proved it to myself.

truly amazing mac and cheese

for the sauce

2 tablespoons unsalted butter

¼ cup (1½ oz/45 g) all-purpose (plain) flour

3 cups (24 fl oz/750 ml) whole milk

1 small yellow onion, thinly sliced

½ bay leaf

pinch of grated nutmeg

kosher salt and freshly ground pepper

½ lb (250 g) macaroni, shells, or other shape

2 tablespoons unsalted butter

1½ cups (6 oz/185 g) mixed grated hard cheeses such as aged Cheddar, Gruyère, and Parmesan

½ cup (4 fl oz/125 ml) heavy (double) cream

serves 4–6

Preheat the oven to 350°F (180°C). Butter a 10-inch (25-cm) square or similar baking dish or 4–6 individual baking dishes.

To make the sauce, in a saucepan, melt the butter over medium heat. Stir in the flour and cook, stirring, until the mixture forms a ball, about 1 minute. Remove from the heat and whisk in the milk, 1 cup (8 fl oz/250 ml) at a time, mixing after each addition until smooth. Return the pan to medium heat and whisk until the mixture comes to a boil. Add the onion, bay leaf, and nutmeg, and season to taste with salt and pepper. Reduce the heat to low, and cook, stirring frequently, until thickened, about 10 minutes. Strain through a fine-mesh sieve into a large bowl and cover to keep warm. You should have about 2½ cups (20 fl oz/625 ml).

Bring a large pot three-fourths full of salted water to a boil, add the pasta, and cook until al dente, according to package directions. Drain, transfer to a bowl, and stir in the butter. Add the sauce, 1 cup (4 oz/125 g) of the cheese, and the cream, and stir to combine. Season to taste with salt and pepper.

Pour the pasta into the prepared dish and sprinkle the remaining ½ cup (2 oz/60 g) cheese over the top. Bake until golden and bubbling, about 30 minutes. Let cool for 5 minutes before serving.

I like the way this sauce pools in the concave pasta rounds known as orecchiette, or "little ears." The sweet roasted squash—a perfect foil for the salty bacon—breaks down a little when it is tossed with the pasta, making the sauce taste really creamy and oh-so-exquisite. This is a favorite dish for serving at causal get-togethers with our friends—it's both impressive and warming, especially on a chilly evening.

roasted butternut and bacon pasta

Preheat the oven to 400°F (200°C). On a rimmed baking sheet, toss together the squash, onion, and oil, then spread it in a single layer. Cut 1 tablespoon of the butter into bits and dot the squash evenly. Season with salt and pepper.

Roast, rotating the pan front to back about halfway through cooking, until the squash and onion are golden and tender, about 45 minutes.

Bring a large pot three-fourths full of salted water to a boil, add the pasta, and cook until al dente, according to package directions. Drain, reserving 1 cup (8 fl oz/250 ml) of the cooking water. Cover the pasta to keep it hot.

While the pasta is cooking, heat a large sauté pan over medium heat. Add the bacon and sauté until most of its fat is rendered and the bacon is crisp on the edges but still chewy at the center, about 4–5 minutes. Pour off all but 1 tablespoon fat and return the pan to medium-high heat. Add the sage and sauté for 30 seconds. Add the squash and cook, stirring occasionally, until heated through, about 2 minutes. Stir in the pine nuts.

Add the hot pasta, the remaining 2 tablespoons butter, and ¼ cup (2 fl oz/60 ml) of the hot pasta water and stir to combine. If the pasta seems dry, stir in a little more pasta water. Season to taste with salt and pepper. Transfer to a warmed serving dish and sprinkle the cheese over the top. Serve right away.

1 butternut squash, about 1½ lb (750 g), halved, seeded, peeled, and cut into bite-sized cubes

½ cup (2 oz/60 g) diced yellow onion

1 tablespoon extra-virgin olive oil

3 tablespoons unsalted butter

kosher salt and freshly ground pepper

½ lb (250 g) orecchiette, penne, or fusilli

4 slices thick-cut apple wood–smoked bacon, chopped

1 tablespoon chopped fresh sage

¼ cup (1½ oz/45 g) pine nuts, lightly toasted

½ cup (2 oz/60 g) grated Parmesan

serves 4–6

Carbonara is so easy to make that it's almost over before it begins. My girls love to watch the alchemy that occurs when the hot pasta is mixed with the eggs and cheese, creating a smooth, thick, creamy sauce. You need to work quickly at this point. If you don't, the eggs will curdle.

spaghetti carbonara

1 tablespoon extra-virgin olive oil

½ cup (2½ oz/75 g) diced pancetta

kosher salt and freshly ground pepper

¾ lb (375 g) spaghetti

2 large eggs

2 tablespoons grated Parmesan cheese

½ cup (2 oz/60 g) grated pecorino romano cheese

serves 4–6

Heat a large sauté pan over medium heat and add the oil. When the oil is hot, add the pancetta and sauté until most of its fat is rendered and the pancetta is crisp on the edges but still chewy at the center, about 4–5 minutes. Remove from the heat and reserve in the pan.

Bring a large pot three-fourths full of salted water to a boil, add the pasta, and cook until al dente, according to package directions.

While the pasta is cooking, in a small bowl, whisk together the eggs until well blended.

Drain the pasta, reserving 1 cup (8 fl oz/250 ml) of the cooking water. Add the hot pasta to the sauté pan, still off the heat, and toss with the pancetta. Add the eggs and stir vigorously to coat the spaghetti strands evenly. Quickly mix in both cheeses. If the pasta seems dry, mix in a little of the hot pasta water to loosen the sauce. Grind pepper generously over the top and season to taste with salt. Toss again and serve at once on warmed plates or bowls.

I prefer Carnaroli rice for making risotto. It holds its texture better and ends up a bit firmer than the more popular Arborio rice. If you can't find Carnaroli, use Arborio, but keep a close watch on the pan to ensure it doesn't get too soft. The finished risotto should be creamy but not soupy.

creamy risotto

In a saucepan, combine the broth and 2 cups (16 fl oz/500 ml) water and bring to a gentle simmer over medium heat. Reduce the heat to the lowest setting to keep the broth at a bare simmer.

Heat a heavy-bottomed saucepan over medium heat and add the butter. When the butter begins to brown, add the onion and sauté until translucent, about 4 minutes. Season with salt and pepper.

Add the rice and sauté until the grains are coated with butter and are hot and translucent, about 3 minutes. Add the wine, bring to a boil, and stir briskly until the wine is absorbed. Add a small ladleful of the hot broth and stir until almost completely absorbed. Continue to add the broth, a small ladleful at a time, cooking and stirring until the broth is nearly absorbed before adding more.

The rice is ready when the grains are almost tender to the bite but still slightly firm at the center and they slide easily over one another when a spoon is drawn through the middle of the pan. This will take about 18 minutes from when you first added the broth. If the rice is not ready, add more broth or hot water and cook for a few minutes longer.

Fold in the cheese and season to taste with salt and pepper. Serve right away. If you have to wait for a few minutes, cover the pan and then thin the risotto with a little hot broth before serving.

3 cups (24 fl oz/750 ml) chicken stock (page 180)

2 tablespoons unsalted butter

½ cup (2½ oz/75 g) finely chopped yellow onion

kosher salt and freshly ground pepper

1 cup (7 oz/220 g) Carnaroli or Arborio rice

1 cup (8 fl oz/250 ml) dry white wine

¼ cup (1 oz/30 g) grated Parmesan

serves 4–6

When you find a food you like, be it bread or cheese, you tend to focus on it. As your obsession takes over, your assessment of the food's characteristics become more nuanced. At our house, we obsess about rice.

Walk into our house on any day and you will find at least six different types of rice in the pantry. We have white and brown basmati, jasmine, long-grain white, Carnaroli, and three kinds of short-grain sushi rice with varying degrees of polish. I call us the house of rice. We eat all kinds all of the time, choosing a specific rice for a specific dish. I gave up trying to use one type of rice for everything after my kids complained that sushi rice didn't taste good with saffron. So now I use long-grain white for Mexican dishes, jasmine for Thai, basmati for Indian and Middle Eastern, and Carnaroli for Italian.

Rice is the perfect flavor chameleon. Cook rice in chicken or vegetable broth to effortlessly boost the flavor. Fold in your favorite vegetables, like asparagus or peas, to the risotto recipe (page 241), or use up your excess herbs, such as parsley, chives, or dill, by mincing them and folding them into any kind of rice at the end of cooking. Cook rice with aromatics such as grated ginger or shredded coconut for a subtlely-scented twist. The more you cook, the more you will find yourself drawn to certain ingredients. As you begin to become more familiar with them, you will seek out your favorites and one day find yourself looking into your cupboard and realizing you have become the house of mustard or flour—or maybe even the house of rice just like us.

A fight ensues between my kids on who will lick the warm, rice-covered spoon when it's pulled from the pot. My youngest rhapsodizes over this smooth, creamy coconut-scented pudding. The aromatic long-grain rice keeps its elegant texture and lends an exotic perfume to the finished dish. The cardamom is a nice companion for the coconut milk, but if you don't have a pod on hand, the pudding is still good without it.

coconut rice pudding

1½ cups (12 fl oz/375 ml) whole milk

3 cups (24 fl oz/750 ml) unsweetened coconut milk

½ cup (4 oz/125 g) sugar

¾ cup (6 oz/185 g) basmati or jasmine rice

½ teaspoon kosher salt

1 green cardamom pod, lightly crushed (optional)

2 large eggs

½ cup (2 oz/60 g) unsweetened dried coconut

Sweetened Whipped Cream (page 278) for serving

serves 4–6

In a saucepan, combine both milks, ¼ cup (2 oz/60 g) of the sugar, the rice, the salt, and the cardamom pod, if using. Bring to a boil over medium-high heat, stirring frequently to prevent the rice from sitting on the bottom and scorching. Reduce the heat to low and simmer uncovered, stirring frequently, until the pudding is thick and creamy and the rice is tender, about 30 minutes.

In a bowl, vigorously whisk together the eggs and the remaining ¼ cup sugar until the mixture falls in a thick, wide ribbon when the whisk is lifted. Add the hot rice, a few tablespoons at a time, to the eggs while stirring vigorously with a wooden spoon.

Transfer the pudding to a single large serving bowl or individual bowls. Let cool to room temperature, then cover and refrigerate until completely chilled.

Meanwhile, preheat the oven to 350°F (180°C). Spread the coconut evenly on a rimmed baking sheet and toast until golden brown, stirring occasionally, about 8 minutes.

Serve the pudding topped with dollops of whipped cream and sprinkled with toasted coconut.

This pilaf covers all of the bases—rice, veggies, chicken—making it a great one-pot meal, and perfect for feeding your family during the week. Don't worry about the small amount of water for the rice; the chicken exudes plenty of juice, and together they are enough liquid to cook the rice.

baked chicken rice pilaf

1 chicken, 4 lb (2 kg), cut into 8 serving pieces

kosher salt and freshly ground pepper

1 tablespoon unsalted butter

1 small yellow onion, finely chopped

2 carrots, finely diced

2 stalks celery, finely diced

2 cloves garlic, minced

1½ cups (10½ oz/330 g) basmati rice

1 teaspoon chopped fresh thyme

1 tablespoon chopped fresh flat-leaf (Italian) parsley

1 bay leaf

serves 4–6

Season the chicken pieces on both sides with salt and pepper. Reserve at room temperature while you start the rice. Preheat the oven to 425°F (220°C).

Heat a large Dutch oven or similar heavy pot with a tight lid over medium-high heat and add the butter. When the butter begins to brown, add the onion, carrot, celery, and garlic, and season with salt and pepper. Cook, stirring occasionally, until the vegetables are tender, about 3–4 minutes. Add the rice and cook, stirring constantly, for 1 minute to toast lightly.

Remove from the heat, stir in the thyme, parsley, and bay leaf, and place the chicken on top of the rice in a single layer. Place in the oven, uncovered, and roast for 15 minutes. Reduce the heat to 350°F (180°C), add 1 cup (8 fl oz/250 ml) water, cover the pot, and bake until the chicken is opaque throughout and the rice is tender, about 45 minutes.

Remove from the oven and let stand, covered, for 10 minutes. Uncover, fluff the rice under the chicken with a large fork, discard the bay leaf, and serve directly from the pot.

I grew up on lentils cooked with a leftover ham bone. When we ate ham, I knew lentils were guaranteed to follow. Here, I have used bacon instead. You can serve the stew as is, or you can spoon it over buttered egg noodles, which is how my daughters like to eat it.

lentil, spinach, and bacon stew

Heat a large saucepan over medium heat. Add the bacon and sauté until most of its fat is rendered and the bacon is golden brown, about 5 minutes. Add the carrot, onion, celery, and garlic, and sauté until tender, 2–3 minutes. Season to taste with salt and pepper.

Add the lentils and stir to coat with the fat. Raise the heat to medium-high, add 3 cups (24 fl oz/750 ml) water, and the stock, thyme, and bay leaf, and bring to a boil. Reduce the heat to medium-low, add 1 teaspoon salt, and simmer, uncovered, until the lentils are tender, 35–40 minutes.

Stir the spinach into the lentil mixture and cook until wilted, about 4 minutes. Season to taste with salt and pepper. Transfer to a warmed serving bowl, sprinkle with the bread crumbs, if using, and serve right away.

3 thick slices bacon, diced

2 carrots, peeled and cut into 1-inch (2.5-cm) chunks

½ small yellow onion, finely chopped

1 celery stalk, chopped

3 cloves garlic, pressed

kosher salt and freshly ground pepper

2 cups (14 oz/440 g) small green French lentils, picked over and rinsed

2 cups (16 fl oz/500 ml) chicken stock (page 180)

1 teaspoon chopped fresh thyme

1 bay leaf

6 cups (8 oz/250 g) baby spinach leaves

Fried Bread Crumbs (page 280), for serving (optional)

serves 4–6

This vegetarian curry is awesome after it sits for a day and the chickpeas have time to absorb the flavor of the spices. I always make it a day ahead of time for just that reason. Spoon this vegetarian curry over hot, steamed basmati rice so you can fully appreciate the flavors in the sauce. If you like a bit of heat, add some minced serrano chile. Serve with spoonfuls of raita (page 65) for a cooling contrast.

chickpea curry

Heat a large saucepan over medium-high heat and add the oil. When the oil is hot, add the onion, garlic, and ginger, and sauté until the garlic starts to brown, 1–2 minutes.

Add the cumin seeds, tomatoes, garam masala, turmeric, coriander, and 2 cups (16 fl oz/500 ml) water, season with 1 teaspoon salt, and bring to a boil. Reduce the heat to medium-low and simmer, uncovered, for 15 minutes.

Add the potatoes and chickpeas, and continue to simmer until the potatoes are tender, 15–20 minutes longer.

Season to taste with salt and mix in the cilantro and lime juice. Transfer to a warmed serving bowl and serve right away. Pass the rice and the raita at the table (see note above).

2 tablespoons canola oil

1½ cups (6 oz/185 g) thin yellow onion wedges

3 cloves garlic, pressed

3 tablespoons peeled, grated ginger

¾ teaspoon cumin seeds

2 cups (12 oz/375 g) fresh or canned diced tomatoes with their juice

2 teaspoons garam masala

½ teaspoon *each* ground turmeric and coriander

kosher salt

2 cups (10 oz/315 g) cubed Yukon gold potatoes

5 cups (35 oz/1 kg) cooked, drained chickpeas (garbanzo beans) (page 281)

¼ cup (⅓ oz/10 g) chopped fresh cilantro (fresh coriander)

2 tablespoons lime juice

serves 4–6

The secret to smooth, creamy hummus is to use fully cooked beans, to add just enough liquid, and to continue to purée until the texture is right. Be careful not to add too much liquid all at once or you risk making soup. White beans can also be substituted for a delicious purée.

hummus with toasted pita

2½ cups (18 oz/500 g) cooked, drained chickpeas (garbanzo beans) (page 281)

¾ cup (7½ oz/235 g) tahini

½ cup (4 fl oz/125 ml) fresh lemon juice

¼ cup (2 fl oz/60 ml) extra-virgin olive oil, plus more for drizzling

kosher salt

½ teaspoon cayenne

3 pita breads, homemade (page 26) or store-bought, each cut into 8 wedges

sweet or smoked paprika for garnish

makes about 3½ cups (28 oz/875 g)

In a food processor, combine the chickpeas, tahini, and lemon juice and process until smooth. If the purée is too stiff to move smoothly, add 1–2 tablespoons of water as needed to achieve a very smooth, thick paste. With the machine running, pour the oil through the feed tube and continue processing until the oil is fully incorporated. Season with 1 teaspoon salt and the cayenne. Transfer the hummus to a bowl, cover, and refrigerate for a few hours to marry the flavors.

Meanwhile, preheat the oven to 350°F (180°C). Place the pita wedges on a rimmed baking sheet, drizzle with oil, and sprinkle with salt. Toast in the oven until golden and crisp, 10–15 minutes. Let cool.

Taste the hummus and adjust the seasoning with salt and/or lemon juice. Transfer to a serving bowl, sprinkle with the paprika, and serve with the pita wedges.

I purée my refried beans until they are smooth. If you like chunky beans, remove a third of the beans, purée the rest, then return them to the pot. Fat is what makes refried beans taste good, and although many shy away from lard for health reasons, it really does make the best refried beans.

refried black beans

Pick over the beans, discarding any that are wrinkled along with any grit. Place in a bowl, add water to cover by 4 inches (10 cm), and soak overnight.

Drain the beans, rinse well, and transfer to a saucepan. Add the garlic, onion, cumin, and water to cover, and bring to a gentle boil over high heat, skimming off any foam that forms on the surface. Reduce the heat to medium-low and simmer for 30 minutes. Add 1 teaspoon salt and water if needed to keep the beans submerged, and continue to cook until the beans are very tender but not mushy, 15–20 minutes longer. Remove from the heat and let the beans cool in their cooking liquid, then drain and reserve some of the cooking liquid. (Or, if not using immediately, refrigerate the cooled beans in the cooking liquid.)

Place the beans in a food processor and process until smooth. If the purée is too stiff to move smoothly, add 1–2 tablespoons of the cooking liquid as needed to achieve a very smooth, thick paste. Taste and season with salt.

Heat a sauté pan over medium heat and add the oil. When the oil is hot, add the beans, stir well to incorporate with the oil, and cook, stirring constantly, until the beans sizzle and pull away from the sides of the pan, about 7 minutes. Taste and adjust the seasoning with salt and add the cayenne if you like your beans spicy. Serve right away.

1 cup (7 oz/220 g) dried black beans

2 large cloves garlic

1 yellow onion, chopped

½ teaspoon cumin seeds

kosher salt

¼ cup (2 fl oz/60 ml) canola oil or ¼ cup (2 oz/60 g) lard

¼ teaspoon cayenne (optional)

serves 4–6

Bittersweet or milk chocolate? Brown or white sugar? Cinnamon, nutmeg, or ginger? That's only the beginning of what the pantry holds.

sugar, spice & chocolate

The world is a sweeter, more aromatic place because of spices, sugar, and chocolate. But it wasn't always that way. At various points in history, each of these ingredients was considered highly valuable, available only to the wealthy. Wars were fought over spice routes. Cane sugar was blockaded by the English. The Aztecs and Mayans were plundered for their cache of chocolate. You can only imagine how dull life was before this delectable threesome was discovered. Today, we take these ingredients for granted, happily spinning them into mile-high soufflés, chewy cookies, creamy puddings, crunchy candies, rich sauces, and crumbly gingerbread, forgetting the historical intrigue and treachery they incited in the hearts of those who wanted them.

Whether it's a big slice of gooey chocolate cake, warm spicy gingerbread, or cinnamon-apple pie that makes you swoon, sugar is ultimately decadent and delicious, especially when paired with spices, chocolate, or fruit.

sweet, sweet sugar

Sugar is a hard worker. It helps stabilize egg whites when you whip up a meringue, makes cakes tender, sweetens coffee or tea, turns into caramel when boiled, is the base for all kinds of icings and confections, and preserves fruits in jam and jelly jars. It has been cultivated in India since 10,000 BC, but it wasn't widely available in Europe until the eighteenth century. Another century would pass before a bowl of white sugar was commonplace on American tables.

Sugarcane and sugar beets are the main sources of the world's sugar, with the latter responsible for only about 30 percent of production. Most of us cannot tell the difference between the two, though there are many bakers who insist on using cane sugar, claiming beet sugar can have an unpredictable effect on their recipes.

Sugar comes brown, raw, and refined. Not surprisingly, the less it is refined, the more nutrition it provides. Moist, soft brown sugar, which is simply granulated sugar that has been colored with molasses, has the greatest nutritional value because of its molasses content. It comes in two styles, dark and light, with the amount of molasses making the difference.

In the United States, so-called raw sugars, which are actually partially refined and range from dark brown to yellow-brown, include Demerara, muscovado, and turbinado. Refined white sugar comes in many crystal sizes, from large sanding sugar (for decorating) to everyday granulated sugar to superfine (caster) sugar to confectioners' (icing) sugar, the latter made by pulverizing the crystals to a very fine powder.

buying and storing sugar

Many conventional and organic sugars are available in supermarkets. Packages that are labeled "pure cane sugar"

guarantee the sugar was extracted from sugarcane. Sacks without the "cane" designation most likely contain sugar made from sugar beets.

Organic sugar, often called evaporated cane juice, must be made from organically grown cane and must be processed and refined organically. Some organic sugars are less refined than others and have a golden cast. But all sugar tastes the same whether it is organic or not.

Store all sugar, regardless of type, in tightly sealed containers to keep it fresh, dry, and free of contaminants. To keep brown sugar soft, refrigerate it. If your brown sugar does harden, heat it in the microwave for about 30 seconds and then use it quickly before it hardens again.

HOW TO CARAMELIZE SUGAR

Caramelizing sugar is easy, but you must be careful. Keep small children and distractions away from the stove. If you are practicing, start with a small amount. When you become confident, move on to larger amounts. Always keep a medium bowl of ice water next to the stove. This is the place to stick any part of you that gets splattered by hot caramel.

1   Pour ¼ cup (2 oz/60 g) granulated sugar into a small, heavy-bottomed saucepan. Heat over medium-high heat while stirring constantly with a wooden spoon. The sugar will begin to melt and lump.

2   Continue to stir until the sugar starts to turn golden. Break up large lumps into smaller pieces with the end of the spoon. They will dissolve as the sugar caramelizes. Stir until the caramel is deep golden brown and all the lumps are gone.

chocolate, a favorite indulgence

Time and again, I have proven to myself that chocolate raises the level of endorphins—those are the natural compounds in your body that flood you with a sense of well-being—in the bloodstream. Perhaps a desire for that endorphin rush was why everyone fought over chocolate centuries ago. Be sure to store chocolate, especially really good-quality chocolate, well wrapped in aluminum foil and plastic wrap, at cool room temperature.

how chocolate is made

Chocolate is made from the pods of the cacao tree, which grows within a narrow geographical band along the equator. Three basic types of cacao tree are cultivated: Forastero accounts for about 80 percent of world production, while Criollo and Trinitario account for about 10 percent each. The finest chocolate comes from the latter two varieties.

After the cacao pods are harvested, the beans and the pulp are removed and fermented in bins for a few days or up to a week. This step is what gives chocolate its familiar taste. The beans are then quickly dried to prevent mold, either in the sun if the weather is good or mechanically if not, and transported to a chocolate manufacturing facility.

The cacao kernels, as the fermented and dried beans are now known, are roasted, shelled, and ground into bits called nibs. The nibs, which contain cocoa solids and cocoa butter, are then mashed into a paste called chocolate liquor, which is the base from which all chocolate is made.

the aroma of spices

Spice production is and always has been very labor intensive. We take spices for granted, but we are not the ones who are harvesting, sorting, hulling, drying, and grinding them. Most spices are grown in tropical regions that stretch from Asia, Africa, and the Middle East to South America, and their harvests have cast a huge aromatic net around the world.

Spices have sweet and savory profiles, with allspice, cinnamon, nutmeg, mace, cloves, ginger, and cardamom among the most common sweet spices and turmeric, caraway, cumin, mustard, celery and mustard seed, and white and black pepper among the most common savory spices. Coriander, fennel, and saffron bridge both the sweet and savory world.

Whole spices usually offer the best quality. Once they are ground, they immediately begin to lose their potency because their aromatic oils have been released. If possible, buy whole spices and grind them yourself with an electric grinder or with a mortar and pestle. Otherwise, buy only small amounts of ground spices so you can use them up quickly. Store all spices—whole and ground—in tightly sealed containers in a cool cupboard. To refresh whole spices

DUTCH-PROCESSED VS NATURAL COCOA POWDER

Dutched or Dutch-processed cocoa powder is unsweetened cocoa powder that has been treated with an alkali to neutralize its acids. It is reddish brown, has a mild flavor, and dissolves readily in liquids. Its delicate taste makes it ideal in baked goods like fine pastries. Because its acids have been neutralized, it cannot be used to activate baking soda (bicarbonate of soda) in recipes, and it cannot be traded out for natural cocoa powder in any recipe that relies on baking soda for its leavening.

Natural cocoa powder is very bitter and imparts a deep chocolate flavor to baked goods, especially brownies and chocolate cakes. It is also acidic, which means it can be used to activate baking soda in recipes.

before grinding, lightly toast them in a 350°F (180°C) oven for a few minutes to release their perfume.

a note on cinnamon

Most cinnamon sold in the United States is cassia, a cousin of true cinnamon. Unlike cinnamon, which is pale tan, thin, rolled quills of inner bark that shatter easily when squeezed, cassia is a dark red-brown, hard, thick rolled bark. True cinnamon is more aromatic and delicate tasting than cassia—and more expensive.

ALL KINDS OF CHOCOLATE

- White chocolate: Despite its name, white chocolate is not true chocolate because it contains no chocolate liquor. It is a mixture of milk solids, cocoa butter, vanilla, and lecithin (an emulsifier). White chocolate is good for icings, fillings, and cookies. I find it too sweet for eating.

- Milk chocolate: Made from milk solids, chocolate liquor, sugar, vanilla, and lecithin, milk chocolate is wonderful for eating out of hand—a candy bar—and in baking when a mellow chocolate taste is desired.

- Dark chocolate: This term is used for a sweetened chocolate—usually semisweet (plain) or bittersweet chocolate—made with chocolate liquor, cocoa butter, sugar, vanilla, and lecithin but without milk solids. In the United States, semisweet and bittersweet chocolates must contain a minimum of 35 percent chocolate liquor, with some containing up to 70 percent. Extra bitter chocolate can be as high as 85 percent chocolate liquor. For baking, I like to use chocolate that contains 60 to 70 percent chocolate liquor because it is not too sweet and rich. Chocolates with higher percentages sometimes contain less emulsifier, which means they can curdle if heated too much.

- Baking chocolate: Also known as unsweetened chocolate, baking chocolate contains chocolate liquor and cocoa butter but no sugar. It provides intense chocolate flavor to baked goods.

- Nibs: These are roasted and ground cacao kernels. They give fillings, cookies, brownies, and other baked goods a chocolaty crunch and are delicious sprinkled over ice cream and frosted cakes.

- Cocoa powder: When nearly all of the cocoa butter has been removed from chocolate liquor, a solid remains that is then ground into this unsweetened powder. Two basic types of cocoa powder are available, natural and Dutch processed (see left).

homemade marshmallow stars

The miracle of homemade marshmallows—the amazing alchemy of gelatin and hot sugar syrup—is a sight to behold. And once you make them, you will never want to buy those jet-puffed marshmallows in plastic bags again.

Watching the ingredients come together is so much fun, we make marshmallows often at our house and give them away as gifts. Our friends wonder what our obsession is. I haven't told them how much fun making marshmallows is because I am afraid I will lose loving homes for our bumper yields.

Making marshmallows is not without risk. Both the hot sugar syrup and the whipping steps—adults-only tasks—can cause burns, so you need to stay focused as you work. Also, be sure to clear away any clutter that might impede your trip from the stove top to the mixer.

marshmallow variations

Mix in the flavoring or color after the marshmallow mixture becomes white and thick.

cocoa marshmallows
Whip in 2 tablespoons unsweetened cocoa powder.

mint marshmallows
Whip in ½ teaspoon pure peppermint extract.

rainbow marshmallows
Dye them any color you want with natural or safe food coloring. Add a few drops until you achieve the color intensity desired.

chocolate-dipped marshmallows

Cut the marshmallows into twelve 1½-inch (4-cm) squares. Dust lightly with confectioners' (icing) sugar, tapping off the excess. Place on a rack on a rimmed baking sheet lined with parchment (baking) paper. Melt 8 oz (250 g) bittersweet chocolate in a double boiler and let cool until warm and still liquid. Ladle the chocolate over the marshmallows, coating as many as you can. Tap the rack against the pan to encourage the excess chocolate to drain off, then refrigerate the marshmallows, still on the rack on the pan, until the chocolate hardens, about 30 minutes. Store the marshmallows in an airtight container at cool room temperature.

what you'll need to make marshmallows

- ¼ cup (1 oz/30 g) cornstarch (cornflour)
- ½ cup (2 oz/60 g) confectioners' (icing) sugar
- 11-by-9-inch (28-by-23-cm) baking pan
- aluminum foil
- canola oil for pan
- 1½ tablespoons unflavored gelatin
- ¼ teaspoon kosher salt
- ¼ teaspoon cream of tartar
- 1¼ cups (10 oz/315 g) granulated sugar
- 1 tablespoon light corn syrup
- 1 teaspoon pure vanilla extract
- 1½-inch (4-cm) star cutter

1 get the pan ready

In a bowl, sift together the cornstarch and confectioners' sugar. Line the pan with aluminum foil, then lightly oil the foil. Sift ¼ cup (1 oz/30 g) of the sugar mixture into the pan, and tilt to coat the bottom and sides. Leave any excess evenly in the bottom.

2 dissolve the gelatin

Pour ½ cup (4 fl oz/125 ml) water into the bowl of a stand mixer. Sprinkle the gelatin over the water, whisk together, then let stand for 5 minutes to soften. Whisk in the salt and cream of tartar. Fit the mixer with the whisk attachment and beat on high speed until fluffy, 2–3 minutes

3 melt the sugar

Put ½ cup (4 fl oz/125 ml) water into a saucepan. Stir in the granulated sugar and the corn syrup. Place over medium-high heat, bring to a boil, and cook, without stirring, until the mixture turns pale tan, about 250°F (120°C) on a candy thermometer, or firm-ball stage.

4 add the hot sugar

Turn the mixer on medium speed
and drizzle the hot sugar syrup
into the gelatin mixture, aiming
it between the beater and the side
of the bowl. Be very careful!

5 whip it

Increase the speed to high and
whip the mixture until it is white
and thick, about 5 minutes. Add
the vanilla and beat until the
mixture cools, about 20 minutes.

6 smooth the
     marshmallows

Pour into the prepared pan. Dip
a palette knife in cold water and
smooth the surface. Let a skin
form on the surface, about 1 hour.
Dust with ¼ cup of the sugar
mixture, and let rest overnight
at cool room temperature.

7 make stars

Line a pan with parchment paper
and dust with the sugar mixture.
Dip the star cutter into the sugar
and cut out marshmallow stars.
Layer the stars in the pan, dusting
with more sugar. Cover tightly
and store at room temperature
for up to 2 weeks.

My daughters like the richness of whole milk in this decadent drink. For less fat, use low-fat milk and omit the cream. For a richer cup, add more cream and less whole milk. The life of a homemade marshmallow is fleeting once it hits the hot chocolate, quickly becoming a pool of foamy marshmallow essence. Stir it in and enjoy.

hot chocolate with marshmallows

4 cups (32 fl oz/1 l) whole milk

½ cup (4 fl oz/125 ml) heavy (double) cream

6 oz (185 g) bittersweet or milk chocolate, or a mixture of both

1 teaspoon pure vanilla extract

¼ teaspoon ground cinnamon (optional)

2–4 tablespoons sugar

marshmallow stars (page 258) for serving

serves 4–6

Pour the milk and cream into a heavy-bottomed saucepan, place over medium-high heat, and heat to just below boiling.

Whisk in the chocolate, vanilla, and cinnamon, if using, and continue to whisk until the milk is frothy and the chocolate is incorporated. Whisk in the sugar to taste.

Divide among warmed mugs and top each serving with one or two plump marshmallow stars. Serve right away.

It's wonderful to serve cupcakes that you've baked from scratch, rather than a mix, for your child's birthday party. Here, I have frosted half of them with vanilla buttercream and half of them with chocolate buttercream to mix it up a bit. For vanilla cupcakes, omit the cocoa powder and melted chocolate, and add an additional ¼ cup (1½ oz/45 g) flour and ¼ cup (2 oz/60 g) sugar.

chocolate birthday cupcakes

1½ cups (7½ oz/235 g) all-purpose (plain) flour

¼ cup (¾ oz/20 g) unsweetened cocoa powder, sifted

1 teaspoon baking powder

½ teaspoon kosher salt

¼ teaspoon baking soda (bicarbonate of soda)

½ cup (4 fl oz/125 ml) whole milk

½ cup (4 oz/125 g) sour cream

½ cup (4 oz/125 g) unsalted butter, at room temperature

1¼ cups (10 oz/315 g) sugar

2 eggs, plus 1 egg yolk

4 oz (125 g) bittersweet chocolate, melted

1 teaspoon pure vanilla extract

makes 16 cupcakes

Preheat the oven to 350°F (180°C). Line 12 cups in one muffin pan and 4 cups in a second pan, spacing the latter around the pan for more even baking, with paper or foil liners.

In a bowl, stir together the flour, cocoa, baking powder, salt, and baking soda. In a bowl, whisk together the milk and sour cream.

In the bowl of a stand mixer, using the paddle attachment, beat together the butter and sugar on high speed until light and fluffy. Stop the mixer and scrape down the sides of the bowl. On medium speed, add the eggs and egg yolk, one at a time, beating well after each addition. Again, scrape down the sides of the bowl. Add the chocolate and vanilla. On low speed, add the flour mixture alternately with the milk mixture, beating after each addition. Scrape down the sides of the bowl. On high speed, beat for 5 seconds to mix well. Spoon the batter into the prepared muffin cups, filling them three-fourths full.

Bake until a toothpick inserted into the center of a cupcake comes out clean, 15–17 minutes. Turn the cupcakes out onto a rack, turn them upright, and let cool completely.

chocolate and vanilla buttercreams

To make the buttercreams, in the bowl of a stand mixer, using the paddle attachment, beat together the butter, confectioners' sugar, and salt on medium speed just until combined. Increase the speed to high and beat until fluffy. Stop the mixer and scrape down the sides of the bowl. Add the milk and vanilla and beat until fluffy. Stop the mixer and measure out 1¾ cups (14 fl oz/430 ml) of the frosting into a bowl and set aside. This is the vanilla frosting.

Sift the cocoa over the remaining frosting in the mixing bowl. Beat on low speed until just combined. Increase the speed to high and beat until fluffy. Add the hot water (to activate the cocoa flavor) and beat the frosting for 1 minute longer. This is the chocolate frosting.

Frost half of the cooled cupcakes with vanilla buttercream and half with chocolate buttercream.

1 cup (8 oz/250 g) unsalted butter, at room temperature

4 cups (1 lb/500 g) confectioners' (icing) sugar, sifted

1 teaspoon kosher salt

¼ cup (2 fl oz/60 ml) whole milk

2 teaspoons pure vanilla extract

¼ cup (¾ oz/20 g) unsweetened cocoa powder

2 teaspoons very hot water

makes about 3½ cups (28 fl oz/875 ml) buttercream

"

My younger daughter was two years old when I was writing my first cookbook. I would put her in her high chair, where she would play with measuring cups and spoons and babble while I tested recipes. One morning, I began to test chocolate cakes. By early afternoon, the kitchen was filled with the scent of warm chocolate. I removed my first try from the oven, and my daughter suddenly fell quiet. I set the imperfectly puffed cake on the counter and started to bake another one. As I leaned over the mixer, I could feel my daughter's eyes boring into my back. Troubled by her silence, I turned to see if she was okay. Sitting perfectly upright, she was intently staring at me and at the cooling cake. Then she began slamming the measuring cups on the high-chair tray and chanting "chocolate cake! chocolate cake!" This from a child who had yet to clearly enunciate a word.

I cut her a sliver, she gobbled it down, and immediately chanted for more. I gave her another slice and then I hid the cake, not knowing how much chocolate was good for a two-year-old. To escape the chocolate-scented air, I quickly hustled her outside to play in the sandbox, where she sat happily making sand cakes and babbling on about chocolate cake. I knew I had just witnessed the birth of a lifelong chocolate lover.

I might have brought out the inner chocolate adoration of my daughter with chocolate cake but these days she and most of her friends are all about cupcakes. My good friend with four kids often skips the frosting and dusts hers with confectioners' (icing) sugar for an easy alternative to going the whole nine yards.

"

Soufflés are spectacular and surprisingly easy to make. At our house, a chocolate soufflé, still dangerously hot from the oven, is pounced on and quickly devoured with big scoops of vanilla ice cream. Just make sure your kids don't burn their tongues. You can assemble this soufflé up to 4 hours in advance and let it sit at cool room temperature until it goes into the oven.

chocolate soufflé

2 tablespoons unsalted butter, plus 1 tablespoon melted for brushing soufflé mold

¾ cup (6 oz/185 g) granulated sugar

6 oz (185 g) bittersweet chocolate, preferably at least 70 percent cacao, chopped

2 tablespoons heavy (double) cream

4 large egg yolks

1 teaspoon pure vanilla extract

6 large egg whites

¼ teaspoon kosher salt

¼ teaspoon cream of tartar

confectioners' (icing) sugar for dusting

serves 4–6

Position a rack in the middle of the oven with plenty of headspace for the soufflé to rise, and preheat the oven to 425°F (220°C). Brush the bottom and sides of a 6-cup (48–fl oz/1.5 l) soufflé mold with the melted butter, and then coat with ¼ cup (2 oz/60 g) of the granulated sugar, tapping out the excess.

In a heatproof bowl, combine the remaining butter, the chocolate, and cream. Set the bowl over (not touching) barely simmering water in a saucepan and heat, stirring occasionally, until melted and smooth. Reserve in a warm place. In a large bowl, vigorously whisk together the egg yolks, vanilla, and ¼ cup (2 oz/60 g) of the granulated sugar until the mixture falls in a thick, wide ribbon when the whisk is lifted. Stir in the chocolate mixture.

In the bowl of a stand mixer, using the whisk attachment, whip the egg whites, salt, and cream of tartar on medium-high speed until foamy. Slowly add the remaining ¼ cup (2 oz/60 g) sugar and whip just until stiff peaks form. Fold the egg whites, one-third at a time, into the chocolate-egg mixture just until combined. Spoon the mixture into the prepared soufflé mold, filling it to the rim.

Bake the soufflé for 15 minutes. Reduce the heat to 400°F (200°C), and continue to bake until the soufflé has risen about 2 inches above the mold rim, 25–30 minutes. Dust the top with the confectioners' sugar and serve right away.

Most kids prefer milk chocolate, and most adults favor dark chocolate. This pudding combines both. Have the kids make the chocolate shavings with a vegetable peeler, or use miniature chocolate chips instead. For a little color and flavor during berry season, add a layer of raspberries.

chocolate-striped pudding cups

4 large eggs

⅔ cup (5 oz/155 g) sugar

4 tablespoons cornstarch (cornflour)

2 teaspoons unsweetened cocoa powder

½ teaspoon salt

4 cups (32 fl oz/1 l) milk

⅛ teaspoon ground cinnamon

1 teaspoon pure vanilla extract

3 oz (90 g) milk chocolate, chopped

2 oz (60 g) bittersweet chocolate, chopped

1 cup heavy (double) cream, well chilled

3 teaspoons sugar

¼ cup (1½ oz/45 g) shaved bittersweet chocolate or miniature chocolate chips

serves 6

In a large heatproof bowl, whisk together the eggs, sugar, cornstarch, cocoa, and salt until blended. In a saucepan, combine the milk and cinnamon and bring to a simmer over medium heat. Slowly pour the hot milk into the egg mixture while whisking constantly.

Return the egg-milk mixture to the pan and cook over medium heat, stirring constantly, until thick and bubbly, 3–4 minutes. Strain the pudding through a fine-mesh sieve into a clean bowl, and stir in the vanilla and both chocolates until melted. Press a sheet of plastic wrap directly on the surface to keep a skin from forming. Cool until warm, then cover and refrigerate until chilled.

Have ready six 1-cup (8–fl oz/250-ml) parfait glasses or one 6-cup (48–fl oz/1.5-l) clear glass bowl.

In a bowl, combine the cream and sugar and whisk until soft peaks form. Layer the pudding and whipped cream evenly in the glasses or the bowl, alternating the pudding and cream to create layers. Top each serving with a dollop of whipped cream and a scattering of chocolate shavings.

It seems like no one can resist the combination of custard and butterscotch, if the speed at which these puddings disappear at our house is any indication. Caramelizing sugar, no matter how small the amount, must be done really carefully and always with adult supervision.

baked butterscotch puddings

Preheat the oven to 350°F (180°C). Place six ¾-cup (6–fl oz/180-ml) ramekins or custard cups in a roasting pan, spacing them apart. In a saucepan, combine the cream and milk and bring to a simmer over medium heat. Remove from the heat and cover to keep warm.

In another saucepan, melt the granulated sugar over medium-high heat, stirring constantly with a wooden spoon, until dark golden brown, 3–4 minutes (see page 255 for tips on caramelizing sugar). Remove from the heat. Working carefully, slowly add the hot cream mixture, a few tablespoons at a time, while whisking constantly. Return the pan to medium heat, and stir until the sugar dissolves and the mixture is smooth. Remove from the heat and keep warm.

In a bowl, whisk together the egg yolks, brown sugar, and salt. Pour the hot caramel cream, one-third at a time, into the yolk mixture while whisking constantly. Strain through a fine-mesh sieve into a pitcher and skim off the air bubbles from the surface with a ladle.

Divide the custard evenly among the ramekins. Cover each ramekin with a flat piece of heavy-duty aluminum foil. Pull the oven rack out halfway, place the pan on the rack, and pour very hot water into the pan to reach halfway up the sides of the ramekins. Push in the rack. Bake until the custards are set but the centers still jiggle slightly when gently shaken, 50–55 minutes. Remove the custards from the water bath. Refrigerate uncovered until cool, then cover and refrigerate overnight. Serve the custards chilled.

2 cups (16 fl oz/500 ml) heavy cream

½ cup (4 fl oz/125 ml) whole milk

¼ cup (2 oz/60 g) granulated sugar

6 large egg yolks

½ cup (3½ oz/105 g) firmly packed brown sugar

¼ teaspoon kosher salt

serves 6

Squares, circles, hearts, and diamonds, whatever the shape, these rich, crumbly, nutty cookies are a treat with tea or cocoa. My girls love to sprinkle the tops with powdered sugar and then place them on the jam-filled bottoms, pressing just hard enough to squish the jam up through the hole. It is a wonderful way to spend an afternoon in the kitchen wrapped in spice.

jammy linzer sandwich cookies

In a bowl, mix together the nuts, flour, semolina, salt, and cinnamon. In the bowl of a stand mixer, using the paddle attachment, beat the butter for 2–3 minutes until creamy. Add the sugar and vanilla and beat until fluffy, 2–3 minutes. Stir in the flour mixture until uniform.

Turn the dough out of the bowl onto a floured workspace. Knead it a few times to incorporate the ingredients. Pat the dough into a disk. Divide the round in half. Roll each dough half between two pieces of parchment (baking) paper to a ⅛ inch (3 mm) thickness. Place on a baking sheet, and chill until firm, about 30 minutes.

Preheat the oven to 350°F (180°C). Remove the dough from the refrigerator one sheet at a time to prevent the dough from getting too soft. Peel off the top sheet of parchment and use it to line a cookie sheet. Using a 3-inch (7.5-cm) cookie cutter, cut the cookies and transfer to the prepared cookie sheet with a metal spatula. When all the cookies are cut, use a small, round ½-inch (12-mm) cutter to cut a hole in the center of half of the cookies for the tops. Gather dough scraps and re-roll between the parchment, chill, and repeat the process.

Bake the cookies for 12–15 minutes until golden on the edges. Cool for 5 minutes on the baking sheet. Transfer the tops to a rack. Turn the bottoms over and spread each with 1 teaspoon of jam. Dust the tops with powdered sugar and sandwich with the bottoms. Layer with parchment in an airtight container and store for up to 1 week.

½ cup (2 oz/60 g) finely ground toasted almonds

¼ cup (1 oz/30 g) finely ground toasted hazelnuts

1½ cups (7½ oz/235 g) all-purpose flour

½ cup finely ground semolina flour

1 teaspoon kosher salt

1 teaspoon ground cinnamon

1 cup (500 g) unsalted butter, at room temperature

½ cup (2 oz/60 g) confectioners' (icing) sugar, plus more for dusting

½ teaspoon pure vanilla extract

1¼ cups (12½ oz/390 g) jam, homemade (page 102) or store-bought

makes about 18 cookies

On cold days, I like to curl up on the couch with a cup of this warm treat and a good book. Toasting the dried spices brings out their essential oils, which gradually fade the longer they are stored. This is a flavor mix I enjoy, but you can vary the amount of each spice according to your taste.

real chai tea

1 teaspoon fennel seeds

3 green cardamom pods, split

8 peppercorns

8 coriander seeds

8 whole cloves

1 cinnamon stick, 4 inches (10 cm) long

2 cups (16 fl oz/500 ml) whole milk

1 tablespoon peeled and thinly sliced fresh ginger

2 tablespoons loose-leaf Assam tea

sugar or honey for serving

serves 4–6

Preheat the oven to 350°F (180°C). Combine the fennel seeds, cardamom, peppercorns, coriander seeds, cloves, and cinnamon in a pie pan and toast until fragrant, about 5 minutes. Pour into a bowl to cool, then crush lightly with the back of a wooden spoon.

In a small saucepan, combine the milk, 2 cups (16 fl oz/500 ml) water, toasted spices, and ginger, and bring just to a boil over medium-high heat. Immediately remove from the heat, cover, and let steep for about 20 minutes.

Return the pan to medium-high heat and bring to a simmer. Remove from the heat, add the tea, cover, and let steep for 3–4 minutes. Strain through a fine-mesh sieve into warmed cups and sweeten with sugar or honey to taste. Serve right away.

get creative

For vanilla chai, split a 1-inch (2.5-cm) piece of vanilla bean and scrape the seeds into the milk mixture when adding the other spices.

For orange chai, add a 3-inch (7.5-cm) orange zest strip to the milk mixture with the spices.

For spiced cocoa, bring the steeped milk mixture to a simmer, strain immediately, and whisk in 3 oz (90 g) bittersweet chocolate, melted, in place of the tea.

This deep, dark gingerbread is deliciously moist and packed with spice. The two gingers, fresh and dried, give the finished cake a big flavor boost. Our family likes to slather the squares with whipped cream, the cool cream delivering a wonderful contrast to the warm spices.

gingerbread

Preheat the oven to 350°F (180°C). Butter an 8-inch (20-cm) square pan and then dust with flour and tap out the excess.

In a bowl, stir together the flour, salt, baking powder, baking soda, ground ginger, cinnamon, and cloves. In a small bowl, stir together the fresh ginger, ½ cup (4 fl oz/125 ml) hot water, and molasses.

In the bowl of a stand mixer, using the paddle attachment, beat the butter and both sugars on high speed until light and fluffy. Stop the mixer and scrape down the sides of the bowl. On medium speed, add the eggs and egg yolk, one at a time, beating well after each addition. Again, scrape down the sides of the bowl. On low speed, add the flour mixture alternately with the molasses mixture, beginning and ending with the flour mixture. Stir in the buttermilk, and then increase the speed to high and beat for 5 seconds to mix well. Scoop the batter into the prepared pan.

Bake until a thin skewer inserted into the center of the cake comes out clean, about 45 minutes. Let cool on a rack. Serve warm or at room temperature directly from the pan.

get creative

For upside-down pear gingerbread, butter the baking dish and line it with pear halves that have been sautéed with brown sugar until caramelized. Top with the batter and bake as directed. Invert the cake onto a platter to serve.

2¾ cups (14 oz/440 g) all-purpose (plain) flour

1 teaspoon *each* kosher salt and baking powder

½ teaspoon baking soda (bicarbonate of soda)

1 teaspoon *each* ground ginger and cinnamon

⅛ teaspoon ground cloves

1 tablespoon peeled and grated fresh ginger

½ cup (5½ oz/170 g) dark, unsulfured molasses

¾ cup (6 oz/185 g) unsalted butter, at room temperature

½ cup (4 oz/125 g) *each* granulated sugar and packed brown sugar

2 eggs, plus 1 egg yolk

½ cup (4 fl oz/125 ml) buttermilk

serves 8

Adults turn into children when they see these homemade pops. They are "soooooo gooood," as my daughter says. I got tired of using the standard freezer-pop molds, so I devised this easier method that doesn't require special equipment. You can also use a 9-inch (23-cm) round cake pan and insert the popsicle stick in the wide curved end of each pop. Or, you can skip the sticks and just scoop it out like ice cream.

orange cream pops

1 qt (1 l) The Best Vanilla Ice Cream (page 71) or store-bought premium vanilla ice cream, softened at room temperature for about 20 minutes

½ cup (4 fl oz/125 ml) frozen organic orange juice concentrate, partially thawed

makes 10 pops

Line a 9-by-7-by-2-inch (23-by-18-by-5-cm) baking pan with plastic wrap, allowing a 5-inch (13-cm) overhang on the long sides.

In a bowl, combine the ice cream and orange juice concentrate and mix until well blended. Pour into the pan and bring the plastic wrap up over the top. Place in the freezer overnight.

The next day, using a sharp knife, cut the frozen ice cream into 10 rectangles (2 rows, 5 rectangles per row). Using a small spatula, lift out each rectangle and insert a wooden popsicle stick into one end. If the pops have softened, lay them on a baking sheet and return them to the freezer until they have firmed up.

Serve directly from the baking sheet, or wrap each pop in waxed paper, twist the paper where the pop meets the stick, and freeze until ready to serve or for up to 1 week.

basics

homemade pastry dough

1¼ cups (6½ oz/200 g)
all-purpose (plain) flour

¾ teaspoon kosher salt

½ cup plus 2 tablespoons (5 oz/155 g) cold
unsalted butter, cut into cubes

½ teaspoon distilled white vinegar

3–4 tablespoons ice water

In a bowl, stir together the flour and salt. Scatter the butter pieces over the flour and cut in with a pastry blender or two kitchen knives until the butter is the size of peas. Add the vinegar, and then gradually add enough of the ice water, stirring and tossing with a fork, until the dough starts to come together. It should be moist but not completely uniform, and its texture will be slightly crumbly.

Turn the dough out onto a lightly floured work surface, press together gently to form a disk 1 inch (2.5 cm) thick, wrap in plastic wrap, and refrigerate for at least 30 minutes or up to overnight. (Or, freeze for up to 3 months, and then thaw, still wrapped, in the refrigerator overnight.)

**makes enough for one single-crust
9-inch (23-cm) pie or one 13-by-4-inch
(33-by-10-cm) rectangular tart shell**

to roll out pastry dough

Dust a work surface lightly with flour. Rolling from the center toward the edges and in all directions, roll out the dough into a 12-inch (30-cm) round about ⅛ inch (3 mm) thick. Work quickly to prevent the dough from getting too warm. Lift and turn the dough a few times as you are rolling to prevent it from sticking. If it starts to stick, dust the work surface with a little flour.

to line a pie pan or tart pan

Lightly dust the rolling pin with flour, and carefully roll the dough around the pin. Position the pin over the pan and unroll the dough, centering it in the pan. Gently lift the edge of the dough with one hand, while pressing it into the edge of the pie pan with another. Trim the edges and proceed as directed in the recipe.

to prebake a pie or tart shell

Preheat the oven to 400°F (200°C). Line a chilled pie crust with a piece of aluminum foil. Fill the foil-lined crust with ceramic pie weights, dried beans, or uncooked rice. Bake the lined crust until it dries out, about 15 minutes. Carefully remove the weights and foil by gathering up the edges of the foil and pulling toward the center, up and out.

For a partially baked crust, continue to bake until the crust is very lightly golden on the edges and dry-looking on the bottom, about 5 minutes longer. Transfer the crust to a wire rack and use as directed in the recipe.

For a fully baked crust, continue to bake until the entire crust is golden brown, about 10 minutes longer. Transfer the crust to a wire rack and use as directed in the recipe.

sweetened whipped cream

¾ cup (6 fl oz/180 ml) heavy (double)
cream, chilled

1 tablespoon sugar

½ teaspoon pure vanilla extract

In a chilled bowl, combine the cream, sugar, and vanilla. Using a whisk, a handheld mixer, or a stand mixer, whip the cream until soft peaks form.

makes 1½ cups (12 fl oz/375 ml)

quick puff pastry

3½ cups (17½ oz/545 g) all-purpose (plain) flour

2 teaspoons kosher salt

1 lb (500 g) cold unsalted butter, cut into
1-inch (2.5-cm) cubes

2 teaspoons white wine vinegar

1 cup (8 fl oz/250 ml) ice water

In the bowl of a stand mixer, stir together the flour and salt. Fit the mixer with the paddle attachment, scatter the butter over the flour mixture, and mix on medium speed until the butter is the size of large peas and coated with flour. On medium-low speed, add the vinegar and then drizzle in the ice water until the flour mixture is moistened and starts to come together. You may not need all of it.

Turn the dough out onto a lightly floured work surface, gather it into a ball, and knead lightly until uniform. Roll out into an 11-by-17-inch (28-by-43-cm) rectangle ½ inch (12 mm) thick. Dust off the excess flour from the surface with a clean, dry dish towel. With a short side facing you, fold the bottom third up and then fold the top third down over it, as if folding a business letter. It should now measure about 6 by 11 inches (15 by 28 cm). If the dough seems warm, wrap in plastic wrap and refrigerate for 15 minutes.

Once again, roll out the dough into a 11-by-17-inch rectangle, ½ inch thick and fold into thirds. Roll and fold one more time. Using the rolling pin, press the folded dough lightly on top to "lock" the folds. Cut the folded rectangle into thirds, wrap each third tightly with plastic wrap, and refrigerate for at least 1 hour or up to overnight. Or freeze for up to 3 months and thaw, still wrapped, in the refrigerator overnight.

makes enough for three 10-inch (25-cm) tarts

easy crème fraîche

2 cups (16 fl oz/500 ml) heavy (double) cream, not ultrapasteurized

¼ cup (2 fl oz/60 ml) buttermilk

In a saucepan, heat the cream until barely warm (95°F/35°C). Pour it into a clean glass jar or bowl and whisk in the buttermilk. Cover with cheesecloth or with plastic wrap poked with lots of tiny holes. (The cream needs oxygen to culture.) Leave at warm room temperature overnight to thicken, then store tightly covered in the refrigerator for up to 2 weeks.

makes 2¼ cups (18 oz/560 g)

vanilla glaze

1 cup (4 oz/125 g) confectioners' (icing) sugar

½ teaspoons kosher salt

2 tablespoons unsalted butter, melted

2 tablespoons whole milk

1 teaspoon pure vanilla extract

In a small bowl, sift together the confectioners' sugar and salt. In a separate bowl, whisk together the butter, milk, and vanilla and stir into the sugar to form a smooth paste. Spread the glaze over warm cinnamon rolls, turnovers, or cakes.

makes ½ cup (4 oz/125 g)

grilled red onion vinaigrette

2 red onion slices, ½ inch (12 mm) thick

3 tablespoons red wine vinegar

½ teaspoon kosher salt

¼ teaspoon sugar

freshly ground pepper

¼ cup (2 fl oz/60 ml) extra-virgin olive oil

Grill the onion slices over a medium-hot fire in a charcoal or gas grill. Chop finely, place in a small bowl, and stir in the vinegar, salt, and sugar. Add a few grinds of pepper, let stand for 10 minutes, and then whisk in the oil, and taste and adjust the seasoning.

makes about ½ cup (4 fl oz/125 ml) vinaigrette

citrus vinaigrette

2 tablespoons fresh orange juice

1 tablespoon *each* fresh lemon and lime juice

1 teaspoon minced shallot

¼ teaspoon kosher salt

freshly ground black pepper

2 tablespoons *each* extra-virgin olive oil and canola oil

2 teaspoons mixed, chopped fresh herbs such as chives, flat-leaf (Italian) parsley, tarragon, and/or chervil, in any combination

In a small bowl, whisk together the orange, lemon, and lime juices; shallot; salt; and 1 or 2 grinds of pepper. Let stand for 10 minutes to allow the flavors to marry. Whisk in both oils, then taste and adjust the seasoning. Add the herbs just before serving to retain their bright color.

makes about ½ cup (4 fl oz/125 ml) vinaigrette

thai lime vinaigrette

¼ cup (2 fl oz/60 ml) fresh lime juice

3 tablespoons fish sauce

1 tablespoon rice vinegar

2 tablespoons brown sugar

1–2 teaspoons thinly sliced serrano chile (optional)

1 clove garlic, pressed

In a small bowl, whisk together the lime juice, fish sauce, vinegar, sugar, chile, if using, and garlic until the sugar dissolves. Let stand for at least 10 minutes to allow the flavors to marry.

makes about ¾ cup (6 fl oz/180 ml) vinaigrette

fried bread crumbs

3 tablespoons extra-virgin olive oil

1 teaspoon minced garlic

¾ cup (3 oz/90 g) plain dried bread crumbs

1 tablespoon chopped fresh flat-leaf (Italian) parsley

1 tablespoon finely chopped lemon zest

kosher salt and freshly ground pepper

In a small frying pan, heat the oil and garlic over medium heat until the garlic starts to turn golden, about 1 minute. Add the bread crumbs and cook, stirring, until golden and fragrant, about 5 minutes. Transfer to a bowl, mix in the parsley and lemon zest, and season with salt and pepper. Use as a garnish on soups or pasta.

makes about ¾ cup (3 oz/90 g) crumbs

flour tortillas

3 cups (15 oz/470 g) all-purpose (plain) flour

2 teaspoons baking powder

1 teaspoon kosher salt

5 tablespoons (2½ oz/75 g) lard, nonhydrogenated solid vegetable shortening, or a mixture, plus more for the pan

1 cup (8 fl oz/250 ml) lukewarm water

In large bowl, stir together the flour, baking powder, and salt. Add the lard and, using a fork or a pastry blender, work the fat into the flour until the mixture is the consistency of fine crumbs. Gradually add the water (it should be just warm to the touch), mixing it in with a fork until the dough is soft but not sticky. If the dough is too firm, work in 1–2 more tablespoons water. Knead the dough for a few minutes until smooth.

Divide the dough into 14 equal pieces, and roll each piece into a ball. Place the balls on a tray, cover with plastic wrap, and let rest at room temperature for 10 minutes or up to 2 hours.

One at a time, dust the balls with flour, flatten in the center with a rolling pin, and roll out on a floured surface into a thin 6-inch (15 cm) round, rolling from the center outward and lifting and turning the round to prevent sticking.

Heat a heavy-bottomed 10-inch (25-cm) frying pan or a griddle over medium-high heat. Lightly oil the pan with lard or shortening and wipe off the excess. (You need to oil the pan for the first tortilla only.) Lay a tortilla across an upturned hand, and then invert your hand, flopping the tortilla flat into the hot pan. Cook for about 30 seconds and then flip the tortilla over. Cook on the other side until the tortilla is slightly puffed and flecked with brown spots about 15 seconds

more. Wrap in a clean kitchen towel and repeat with the remaining tortillas, stacking them as they are ready. Serve right away.

Store leftover tortillas in a resealable plastic bag in the refrigerator for up to 5 days. To rewarm the tortilla, remove from the bag, wrap in aluminum foil, and heat in a 250°F (120°C) oven until warm.

makes 14 flour tortillas

cooking dried beans

1 cup (7oz/220 g) dried beans, such as chickpeas, cannellini, or black beans

4 large cloves garlic

kosher salt

Pick over the beans, discarding any that are wrinkled, along with any grit. Place in a bowl, add cold water to cover by 4 inches (10 cm), and soak overnight.

Drain the beans, rinse well, and transfer to a saucepan. Add the garlic and water to cover by 4 inches. Bring to a gentle boil over high heat, skimming off any foam that forms on the surface. Reduce the heat to medium-low and simmer for 40 minutes. Add 2 teaspoons salt and water if needed to keep the beans submerged and continue to cook until the beans are tender but not mushy, about 30 minutes to 1½ hours longer, depending upon the beans.

Remove from the heat and let the beans cool in their cooking liquid, then drain and reserve some of the cooking liquid. Use at once, or, if not using immediately, refrigerate the cooled beans in their liquid in an airtight container for up to 1 week.

makes about 2½ cups (18 oz/560 g) cooked beans

how to...

toast nuts and coconut

Most nuts taste better if you toast them before you use them in a recipe. Toasting helps crisp them, reduce their bitterness, and brings out their flavor. Make sure to toast nuts just before you are ready to use them.

Preheat the oven to 325°F (165°C). Spread the nuts or shredded dried coconut in a single layer on a half-sheet pan and toast, stirring occasionally for even browning, until fragrant and the color deepens. Watch them carefully as the timing varies depending on the type or the size of the nuts. Most nuts take 10–20 minutes; shredded coconut will take 5–10 minutes.

skin nuts

To skin hazelnuts, peanuts, or walnuts, first toast the nuts, then pour the still warm nuts into a kitchen towel and rub the nuts firmly. Peel away any stubborn bits with your fingers.

To skin almonds or pistachios, place the nuts in a heatproof bowl, add boiling water to cover, and let the nuts stand for about 1 minute. Drain, rinse with cold water, and squeeze each nut between two fingers to remove the skin.

melt chocolate

Place chopped chocolate in a heatproof bowl that fits snugly in the rim of a heavy saucepan. Fill the saucepan with water to a depth of about 1½ inches (4 cm) and heat over low heat until it barely simmers. Place the bowl with the chocolate over (not touching) the water. Heat, stirring often with a heatproof rubber spatula, until the chocolate melts. Remove the bowl and set aside to cool slightly before using.

zest citrus

The best tool for zesting citrus is a Microplane fine grater. Hold the clean citrus fruit in the palm of your hand and pull the grater across the fruit, following the contour, and removing only the colored portion of the fruit. The white pith beneath is bitter. Tap the Microplane firmly on the side of the bowl to release the zest. If you don't have a Microplane or zester, you can remove the zest with a vegetable peeler and then finely mince the zest with a sharp knife.

hull strawberries

Insert a paring knife at a slight angle into the stem end of the berry. Rotate the knife until the stem is free, then lift out the stem and core.

peel peaches and tomatoes

Bring a saucepan three-fourths full of water to a boil over high heat. While the water is heating, cut a small, shallow X in the bottom of the peach or tomato. Drop it into the boiling water and leave for 30 seconds. Remove the peach or tomato with a slotted spoon. When it's cool enough to handle, starting at the X, peel the skin from the fruit.

pit stone fruit

Starting at the stem end, use a small, sharp knife to cut the fruit in half lengthwise, cutting around the large, central pit. Grasping each half, rotate the halves in opposite directions and pull apart. Pluck out the pit with your fingers or use the knife to dislodge it. If the halves don't want to rotate, you can cut slices away from the pit, then just discard the pit.

core apples and pears

If the recipe calls for peeled apples or pears, first peel the fruit with a vegetable peeler. Cut the fruit in half lengthwise through the stem. Use a melon baller to remove the seeds and a paring knife to remove the core and stem ends.

clean a leek

Trim the dark green leaves off the top of the leek. You can add these to some carrots and celery to make a nice vegetable stock, or discard. Cut the leek in half lengthwise, keeping the root intact. Rinse under cold water, making sure to get all of the dirt from between the leek layers. Slice as directed in the recipe.

blanch vegetables

Blanching is used to cook vegetables partially or all the way to tenderness. Partial cooking in advance can help speed the final steps of meal preparation. Bring 3 to 4 quarts of water to a boil and add 1½ tablespoons per quart of water. Ready a large bowl of ice water for the blanched vegetables. Add the vegetables to the pan and cook to the desired tenderness, 3–8 minutes depending on the vegetable. Remove the vegetables with a slotted spoon, cool quickly in the ice water, then drain well.

peel hard-boiled eggs

Remove the pan containing the cooked eggs from the heat. Drain the eggs then run cold water over the eggs to cool slightly. Tap the eggs against the side of the pan to break the shells and then fill the pan with cold water and let the eggs sit for 30 minutes. If the water gets warm, drain and refill with cold water. Drain the eggs and peel. The cool water slips between the shell and the cooked egg making shell removal easy.

IDEAS FOR MEALS

Classic Dinner: Herbed Garden Salad with Goat Cheese, Grilled 5-Spice Pork Chops, Chunky Applesauce, Creamiest Mashed Potatoes, Apricot Crumble

Make Ahead Supper: Veggie Minestrone, Baked Chicken Rice Pilaf, Baked Butterscotch Puddings

A Dinner for Kids to Cook: Pizza Pizza Pizza, Herbed Garden Salad with Goat Cheese, Orange Cream Pops

Summer Brunch: Stacks of Blueberry Pancakes with maple syrup, Dry-Cured Bacon, A Colorful Frittata, Tropical Smoothies

Winter Brunch: Banana–Brown Sugar Muffins, Good Morning Scramble, Blood orange wedges, Hot Chocolate with Marshmallows

Tea Party: Cream Scones, Lemony Lemon Bread, Toasty Almond–Cherry Turnovers, Jammy Linzer Sandwich Cookies, Real Chai Tea

A Big Birthday Meal: Oven-Fried Chicken Fingers, Crispy Cornmeal Fish with Tartar Sauce, Truly Amazing Mac and Cheese, Chocolate Birthday Cupcakes with Chocolate and Vanilla Buttercreams

South of the Border Dinner: Corn Fritters with Lime, Fish Tacos with Slaw, Corn Tortillas, Refried Black Beans, Chocolate Striped Pudding Cups

Middle Eastern Feast: Lamb Kebabs with Pita, Cool-as-a-Cucumber Raita, Tabbouleh, Coconut Rice Pudding

An Indian Dinner: Chickpea Curry, Cool-as-a-Cucumber Raita, Steamed rice, Mango slices

index

Oxmoor House

OXMOOR HOUSE

Oxmoor House books are distributed by Sunset Books
80 Willow Road, Menlo Park, CA 94025
Telephone: 650-321-3600 Fax: 650-324-1532

VP and Associate Publisher Jim Childs
Director of Marketing Sydney Webber

Oxmoor House and Sunset Books are divisions of
Southern Progress Corporation

WILLIAMS-SONOMA, INC.

Founder & Vice-Chairman Chuck Williams

FAMILY MEALS

Conceived and produced by Weldon Owen Inc.
415 Jackson Street, San Francisco, CA 94111
Tel: 415-291-0100 Fax: 415-291-8841
www.weldonowen.com

In Collaboration with Williams-Sonoma, Inc.
3250 Van Ness Avenue, San Francisco, CA 94109

A Weldon Owen Production
Copyright © 2008 Weldon Owen Inc.
and Williams-Sonoma, Inc.

First printed in 2008
10 9 8 7 6 5 4 3 2

ISBN-13: 978-0-8487-3263-9
ISBN-10: 0-8487-3263-4

Printed in Singapore by Tien Wah Press

WELDON OWEN INC.

Executive Chairman, Weldon Owen Group John Owen
CEO and President Terry Newell
Senior VP, International Sales Stuart Laurence
VP, Sales and New Business Development Amy Kaneko
Director of Finance Mark Perrigo

VP and Publisher Hannah Rahill
Executive Editor Kim Laidlaw

VP and Creative Director Gaye Allen
Senior Art Director Emma Boys
Designer Lauren Charles

Production Director Chris Hemesath
Production Manager Michelle Duggan
Color Manager Teri Bell

Photographer Ray Kachatorian
Illustrator Rosie Scott
Food Stylist Lillian Kang
Prop Stylist Lauren Hunter
Photographer's Assistant Chris Andre
Photo Shoot Assistant Molly McCulloch

ACKNOWLEDGMENTS

From Maria Helm Sinskey: The book was nurtured from inception
to completion by a group of people dedicated to good food and
shared experience. Thank you to Tory Ritchie who brought my
name to the attention of Hannah Rahill. To the crazy shoot team
of Emma Boys, Kim Laidlaw, Ray Kachatorian, Chris Andre, Lillian
Kang, mellow Molly McCulloch, and to Gaye Allen who got us out
of the house and out to dinner. Never on this planet has so much
fun been had while working on a project we all loved so dearly.
My family deserves a big thanks, my daughters Ella and Lexi who
sometimes smiled through tears to get the job done and my
ever-so-patient husband Rob, who let me do it my way most of the
time. A second thanks to Kim, who edited patiently, and retained
a good sense of humor throughout the entire process. And last but
not least, a big thank you to Fred Hill, my agent and friend, who
never falters in his belief that I will get it done.

Weldon Owen would like to thank the following individuals for their
kind assistance in making this book a reality: Ken DellaPenta, Leslie
Evans, Anna Giladi, Carolyn Keating, Sharon Silva, and Tuan Tran.